Lessons *with* Margot

LESSONS
with
MARGOT

Notes on Dressage from the author of
THE DRESSAGE CHRONICLES

KAREN MCGOLDRICK

Deeds Publishing | Atlanta

Copyright © 2017 — Karen McGoldrick

ALL RIGHTS RESERVED—No part of this book may be reproduced in any form or by any electronic or mechanical means, including information storage and retrieval systems, without permission in writing from the authors, except by a reviewer who may quote brief passages in a review.

Published by Deeds Publishing in Athens, GA
www.deedspublishing.com

Printed in The United States of America

Cover photo by Ashley Marascalco; cover design by Mark Babcock
Text layout by Mark Babcock

Library of Congress Cataloging-in-Publications data is available upon request.

ISBN 978-1-947309-13-5

Books are available in quantity for promotional or premium use. For information, email info@deedspublishing.com.

First Edition, 2017

10 9 8 7 6 5 4 3 2 1

Dedication

This book is dedicated to my many "Margots." I hesitate to try and name all of you for fear of leaving someone out, but want you to know that there is nothing that can compare to those hours in the saddle under your direction where you let me know that I was worthy of your attention and that my horse, no matter how limited, was a "good" horse.

Then there are the "Margots" who never knew I was watching and listening. Some I have only met in books and videos. I was reading, listening, watching, and trying my best to let their wisdom and skill inhabit my riding. I am grateful to them, too.

To all my "Margots" my hope is that I can pass on to other riders and horses, some measure of what you have given me.

"Riding a horse is not a gentle hobby, to be picked up and laid down like a game of solitaire. It is a grand passion. It seizes a person whole and once it has done so, he/she will have to accept that his life will be radically changed."

—Ralph Waldo Emerson

Contents

Introduction   1
Preface   5

Part One: Basics   11
Resources   11
The Nature of Horses   22
Horses: Why do we love them so?   24
Oh, the Mystery of it All   25
A Word about Position   31
A Word About Control   36
Notes on Learning and Teaching   38
A Word About Connection   45
Testing Correct Connection — The Stretch Down Exercise   48
Testing Correct Connection — Überstreichen   49
A Word About Lightness   50
Building Your Dressage Horse From Scratch   52
The Starfish story (Author unknown)   56

Part Two: Speaking a Common Language   57
Installing the Controls   57
The Controls: Longitudinal   58
The Controls: Lateral   59
Balance, Suppleness and Strength   62
Half-halts   68
Examples of Half-halts: Longitudinal and Lateral   70
Vocabulary of Dressage and the Training Scale   74

Part Three: Putting it Together   77
Notes on the Progression of the Exercises   77
Review of the Exercises   78
Leg Yielding   78

Shoulder-In	80
Counter-Canter	85
Flying Change	89
Turn On the Haunches/Walk Pirouette	96
Collected, Medium, Extended Gaits, Plus Rein-Back	100
Notes on Piaffe	101
Notes on Passage	104
More Notes on Medium and Extended Gaits	106
Notes on the Rein-Back	107
Notes on Neck Position	109
Notes on Haunches-In (Travers), Haunches-Out (Renvers) and Half-Pass	110
Notes on Counter Change of Hand/Zigzags in Half-Pass	112
Notes on the Halt	114
Canter Pirouettes	116
Part Four: Commitment to Excellence	**123**
Catching the Corners	123
Remember the Center Line (And All Those Other Lines)	126
Evaluating Progress	129
Going Deeper into the Exercises	131
Taking It On The Road	135
Discipline: The Secret Sauce	145
Speed Bumps, Road Blocks, and Heartbreaks	148
A Word About Insurance	153
What's It's All About?	153
If I Can't be Riding	156
Self Examination/Mental Game	158
Acknowledgments	**161**
About the Author	**163**

Introduction

This book is not intended to be a complete training "manual." It is instead an attempt to share with my readers a synthesis and rational organization of the best parts of my dressage riding education into a digestible form. If you were a reader who enjoyed the riding and training and teaching scenes from my novels, this book should, I hope, also be of some benefit: both educational and entertaining.

I use my own voice throughout, but know that nothing I say or note is original. Instead, what I pass along to my readers is what has been given to me. Like a lot of American horsemen and women, my education progressed in less than straight line; I made some zigs and zags, some productive, some less so. But along my path I had some wonderful instruction that "stuck" with instructors both famous and not so famous.

I had years where I was the riding clinic Queen, signing up for everything. And because I already had a firm foundation as a rider and the instruction was with qualified clinicians, those clinics never confused me (we have had wonderful clinicians come to our area.). I felt that if I came away from a clinic with a new exercise, or a new way of thinking about some aspect of training and riding, then the money was well spent.

The clinics also served to give me practice riding in front of an audience, while receiving constructive criticism. Clinics and symposiums are excellent places to find like-minded riders. I valued the camaraderie I found by attending these events. I also volunteered to be a demonstration rider every chance I got. This was not always "comfortable" but it was always beneficial.

In addition to riding, I have audited countless clinics, symposiums, scribed at shows, gone through the "L" program (multiple times), and the USDF Instructor/Trainer program, first as an organizer and demo rider and then as a instructor/trainer. My participation in that program spanned over fifteen years. In the pursuit of learning, I have gone three times to Germany to ride. I also attended Olympic Games and World Cups and other championships as an enthusiastic spectator both here and abroad. Of course, I also competed, which was fun (when I was doing well) and not much fun when I was having mishaps or struggling. But, I learned to "take the wild ride" and laugh myself silly with my fellow competitors regardless of the day's results. Being obsessed with the sport drove me to try to learn through my reading, seeing, hearing, and from the seat of my pants in the saddle. Along the way, I found friends; talented, quirky, intelligent, one-of-a-kind, kick-ass friends.

Then there are my mentors. Those relationships I have cherished. The mentoring I received and the friendships that developed became core to my development as a rider, teacher, trainer, and human being. Some have been there to hold my hand while I cried, or to cheer me on when got a spot in a victory gallop, or simply a clean flying change. There is a short list of people I trust completely and can if need be lean on reliably for wisdom and genuine concern, and those relationships are priceless.

I tend to slip into the naive assumption that I am "about" the same age as my friends at the barn; what an absurd falsehood that is. I am at this writing sixty years old. My back sometimes gives me fits (I have severe spinal stenosis). Injections have calmed things down, and fortunately my current horse is very comfy to sit. But, despite the fact of my age, and my aches and pains, I look forward to my rides every day and, on a good day, I think I'm actually improving.

It's been six years now since I published my first installment of my four novels called "The Dressage Chronicles." I hope I have contributed something of value to the body of literature on dressage. This companion non-fiction volume should finalize the series. I hope as you read the following, both the personal and technical passages, that you hear the voice of Margot, and Deb, Emma and Natalie and, of course, Lizzy.

Preface

On one of my trips to my home state of California I pointed out to my husband the "Der Wienerschnitzel" fast food restaurant that still stands on the corner of Phillips Road and Foothill Blvd. There used to be a dusty community riding arena on Phillips Road. My friends and I would ride to the arena, "work" our horses, and then ride through the drive- thru of Der Wienerschnitzel to buy our hot dogs and eat them while we rode home. My husband was shocked—and so was I looking at the traffic whizzing along on Foothill Blvd.

In those days, no one wore a helmet. Mobile phones had not yet been invented. My friends and I rode our bikes to the horses and managed to be home in one piece in time for supper. Those horses were saints, and I suppose our parents understood that. The pony I rode was also used for vaulting. It was on "Sonny-Boy" that I earned my vaulting bronze medal. I recall decorating Sonny and with my friend, Erica, on her horse, Joaquin, riding down into the village of Claremont, California, to be part of our town's Fourth of July parade. We were dressed up as Romeo and Juliet—I was Romeo. My mother made my costume. Why we went "Shakespearean" for the Fourth of July, I can't recall.

The way we kept horses can hardly be believed today. I did not know anyone who had a proper barn (although they did exist elsewhere in Southern California). Those in my area who were upscale had "pole pens," those who were not so fancy had pens made of wood. Over one corner of the pen was always a section of metal roofing. Southern California is very hot and shade is essential. On the fence was usually hung a metal barrel that had been cut out to serve as a hay rack. The hay went in the top, and the grain went in the bottom. Rocks were cleared from the ground (it was very rocky soil) but bedding was unheard of. Manure was pushed out the rear of the pen and then pushed away into a pile where it was baked by the hot sun. We had no fly system.

It was hot as Hades in the summertime but there were no fans, because there was no electricity at the pens. Once my wooden tack locker was broken into and my saddle was stolen. I had a stretch where I simply rode bareback until my grandmother sent me a check for a saddle. I make it sound like the poor kid who had to walk uphill both ways to school. But I was lucky. I was riding and, while I didn't realize it, I was developing balance and suppleness on the back of a horse in the most natural way.

Even then I dreamed of better things. My Dad took me to tour the famous Flintridge Riding Club in Pasadena as prospective members (we never could have afforded it). He also took my mom and me occasionally to Santa Anita racetrack, the Forum International Horse Show, and Cal Poly Arabians Saturday demonstrations for the public. And my wonderful first instructor took me along to audit the monthly dressage lectures and clinics sponsored by the Pomona chapter of CDS (California Dressage Society). Occasionally, we also attended events at the Los Angeles chapter of CDS.

In those days, Hilda Gurney was developing her famous horse, "Keen," under the regular guidance of Franz Rochowansky. I felt special when Hilda one time allowed me to hand-graze her horse, "Didit," while she rode Keen. Another time, a rider allowed me to ride her stallion around at a walk while they went out for coffee! These were such highlights for me that they are still vivid in my memory. Between DeKunnfy and Rochowansky, I at least became familiar with dressage terminology.

But, what I yearned to do at that time was run and jump. We had plenty of "firebreak" roads in the foothills and a flat plateau near where I rode, and both those places offered great places for a gallop. Once I owned my first horse (an off-the-track racehorse who was way too much for me), I got to experience my first real gallop. On weekends, Erica and I sometimes packed lunches and tried to ride to the snowline, spending long hours on horseback.

The local arena offered gymkhanas where our patient horses were asked to do crazy stuff. Erica and I were pretty good at rescue race because Joaquin rode double and, although I'm not sure I ever won the "Dollar Bill Marathon," I got pretty close a couple of times. The Boot Race involved everyone taking off one boot and making a pile of them at the end of the arena. We ran our horses to the pile, jumped off, put on our missing boot, jumped back on and raced to the finish line. Half the horses usually ran off before their riders could mount. It was chaos. At around that time I was also a member of Equestrian Trails Incorporated, Corral #45. I even served one year as junior president.

While I would not recommend coming up in the horse world exactly the way I did, when I look back there were some benefits; one being that my friends and I spent so much time with our horses and on our horses that we learned about balance and gained suppleness by osmosis.

All it takes to break the blissful bubble of ignorance is to see riding and horses that exist on a level so above your own that your low status feels painful. My little equine friend, who had allowed me to stand on his back and also eat a hot dog while I walked on loose reins down the side of a road, looked like a yak compared to the horses at the dressage clinics. It makes me a little sad now to remember when that little "yak" of a pony was rejected in my mind as not good enough. But I had also become dissatisfied with my level of skill, too. I had seen myself riding in home movies. I was horrified, and I was hungry. I wanted more.

Sonny Boy | Owner: Mora Celaya
While no beauty, this little guy allowed me to trek up and down hills, through ravines, as well as through the drive through lane at Der Weinershnitzel

We Betcha, off the track Thoroughbred | Owner: Karen Jaffa (McGoldrick)
Humble does not adequately describe the housing where my "Betsy" was kept. Trash cans for water, oil drums for hay and feed. There was no electricity, no fly control, and no bedding. Grass simply did not exist naturally in the arid climate of Southern California without irrigation systems. Regardless, I had a horse (and evidently an admirer).

Part One: Basics

Resources

Life is not fair. All horses are expensive, and horses bred specifically for the sport, especially if they have had good training, are *very* expensive. Paying for instruction may seem out of reach. Yet, I know amazing horsemen who came from nearly nothing. And there they are; some of them in the "big" arena. How did they do that?

The truth is we all tend to look ahead of us and see what we are lacking rather than remembering to occasionally look behind us and understand how far we have come. So, thanks for bearing with me as I share more of my humble beginnings and then fast forward to the present.

I once had someone tell me that I was living "their" dream. I was struggling at that point with something so important that today I can't tell you what it was. But I have never forgotten her words which, at the time, "woke" me up.

Every rider has a story how they came to be where they are. The same can be said for every horse. I never had to reach far to find a story for the characters who inhabit *The Dressage Chronicles* because inspiration for most of them were close at hand. I have observed relentless work ethic, obsessive drive to improve, and a deep and abiding love of the horse in the best of those riders I admire. I also have witnessed a durable sense of humor and depend on it myself, because horses have an unfailing skill to "keep it real" and nothing eases a bruised ego better than a good belly-laugh.

When I was young, I harbored a vain fantasy that I would be "discovered" like some movie star sitting at a lunch counter. I'm embarrassed to admit it now. But, it didn't take me long to figure out that wasn't going to happen. While someone may give you encouragement, gaining the knowledge and skill is something no one will "give" you. The responsibility is all yours. In that regard, we are all self-taught. And those who do not take on the responsibility are nearly unteachable.

There were no proper "barns" in the college town where I grew up in Southern California. There were "ranches" further out, but they were all too far away. So, the only riding I was able to do was some trail riding with a friend who had a horse in Chino and would take me along. I loved it, but it was not a daily thing, and besides, it was done in a western saddle, and I had already decided that I wanted to ride "English" since I had been reading a book called *School for Young Riders*, written by Jane Marshall Dillon. The book had short quizzes at the end of each chapter. I read the book repeatedly, taking the quizzes until I could score 100% on all of them. I lived the story along with the protagonist (who was based on real-life rider Kathy Kusner). I was ready to move to Virginia to ride with Jane Marshall Dillon; heck, I was ready to be the star in her next book.

It was a fluke, really, to spot an ad in our community newspaper for a working student position a short (but uphill) bike ride from our home. The woman didn't expect a twelve- year-old to answer her ad, but she kindly took me on. She had just earned her British Horse Society Assistant Instructor Certificate while on a sabbatical year in England and she was looking for a "guinea pig" student. She had a tiny backyard "arena" (without any footing) and four kind-hearted grade horses. But, she had a desire to teach, and I had a desire to learn.

My formal education began with this instructor and the British Horse Society Pony Club manuals. Not a bad way to start. She also was a member of the California Dressage Society, Pomona Chapter. I went with her to the monthly lecture and clinics given by Charles Dekunffy, at Cal Poly, and was enthralled by his lectures and lessons. My early years did ultimately include a shift toward the Hunters, and I did get to Virginia for college to learn the Littauer system of riding hunters. (It was the same system that I had first read about in Jane Marshall Dillon's book.) My Sweet Briar years included Foxhunting and Combined Training, and even Hunt Meet Pair Racing. It also included classroom study of the horse. Those were four magical years where I earned a degree in English and Creative Writing and met my husband who was a student at the University of Virginia. My roommate at Sweet Briar was also a rider, became my dearest friend, and the two of us are still riding. (She found us a summer job working at Shakerag Hounds Hunt Club in Suwanee, Georgia. We hound-walked, exercised hunt and polo horses, and even got to go out cub-hunting. It was an unforgettable summer. Strangely enough, this California girl eventually found herself moving to nearby Alpharetta.)

It's been said that the three things every successful dressage rider needs are "Time, Talent and Money," but it is the rare person gifted with an abundance of all three. Most of us are always feeling the lack of one or more of them. I can add to that list another essential element: "A Horse."

A rider without a horse is no longer a rider; they are a pedestrian. If you know and love words like I do, you know that "pedestrian" not only refers to someone on foot, it also means ordinary. When we ride, we are lifted off the ground, we are no longer ordinary. When you are grounded, life feels mundane. A rider must have a horse to ride; it's as simple as that. The periods of my life where I have been "grounded" have been blessedly short (and were not suffered with grace.)

Riding schools with their string of lesson horses have become increasingly rare, which is a shame. The high cost of keeping and maintaining a lesson horse has sadly made this business model untenable in most parts of the country.

But "where there is a will, there is a way." A stubborn determination to find a horse to ride, no matter what, seems to be part and parcel of the equestrian personality. I have found that there are many horse owners who struggle to pay their board, or struggle to find enough time to give their horse daily exercise. These situations provide opportunities for half-leases, sharing the burden of the high cost of horse ownership. If these leases are under the supervision of a good instructor, then the horse is protected by the instructor's supervision of the rides, which provide reassurance for the horse's owner. When these arrangements work out I have seen real friendships develop where all benefit. When they don't work out, they can be a source of conflict.

Finding these opportunities means networking since half-leases are rarely advertised. Relationships such as these require a level of trust and comfort between all parties. Not only must the owner and trainer be comfortable with the skill level of the lessor, the horse must agree to the arrangement, too. I have been fortunate to have always found horses to ride, even when I was horseless. Whether I used school horses, leased horses or was lucky to be given rides on horses through working off the rides with barn work, I found a ride.

Still, nothing can match having a horse of your own. And although we should purchase the best and most appropriate horse for our needs, we all are limited by what we can afford. But sometimes, what you have, rather than what you wish you had, turns out to be a blessing in disguise. Being "stuck" with a less than "fancy" horse gave me the opportunity to go through the levels, making my mistakes on a quiet and forgiving soul, without anyone tsk-tsking my being "overmounted." No one was jealous—but ultimately some people were surprised or even impressed at my "silk purse from a sow's ear" project.

I like to tell people about my first dressage horse, "Bodacious," who will forever hold a place in my heart. I bought him as a two-year-old for $900.00. He was a registered Quarter Horse, but looked more like a Thoroughbred. At the time of his purchase I intended to train him as a children's hunter and sell him. He was initially my project horse, bought to entertain myself while my husband was in law school. I kept him at a stable a few miles outside town, where by bringing in the horses at night and dropping feed, I paid a reduced board. As I recall, that made my board bill $60.00/month.

Bodacious, Quarter Horse | Owned by Karen Jaffa McGoldrick
Bodacious was my first opportunity to train a horse for myself, having purchased him when he was two years old for $900. His gaits were limited, but his patience was endless as I made course corrections along our path. He was my dear pet as well as my riding partner. He will forever hold a place in my heart.

He was sweet and sensitive with large "doe-eyes." I worked with a hunter coach when I could scrape up a few extra bucks (I had a job, but we also were living on student loans). Some of the other boarders were event riders, and they had built jumps along our trails, so he went over those obstacles, too. I trained him "by the book" which in those days meant the Littauer system I had learned at Sweet Briar College. I was almost surprised to find Bodacious followed the system easily.

Bo's one fault was he was a terrible shipper. Partly it was due to the fact that I did not own a trailer so had little opportunities to work with him. All his life he was a "scrambler" and I always had to be careful on left turns with him. If I was the driver he did better than if someone else drove. No one else crept through those turns as slowly as I did.

The last summer of law school my husband had a clerkship in Atlanta, and I found a job exercising foxhunting horses in the afternoons for the field master of Shakerag Hounds. This particular barn also evented, and when they had a dressage clinic I signed up for it, borrowing a dressage saddle. When I look at the photos now I laugh at the short stirrups, but I remember thinking at the time that they were uncomfortably long.

After my clinic, I began taking dressage lessons along with my jumping lessons. For a lark, I signed up for a local dressage show. I won all four of my Training level classes. I had never been that successful at a hunter show before, and took it as a sign. At the time, I thought if I advanced as far as Second level, I would be satisfied.

Bodacious instead went up the levels in a slow but steady way. I took a "remedial year" at Second level, as so many do, because the concept of collection was completely foreign after my four years of riding hunters at Sweet Briar. I also had to learn how to train straight, clean, and balanced flying changes that happened on my aids.

Bodacious ultimately learned to make flying changes every stride. He learned to make modest piaffe and passage steps, too. What he never could do was extended trot. His trot was limited in scope, and the hard lesson I learned was that by running him onto his forehand in an effort to get more length of stride, I damaged his suspensory ligament. He came back from the injury after a nine-month rest. But I shed many guilty tears over my mistake.

Bodacious taught me many other important lessons, he was by chance, the right horse to have in my life at the beginning of my dressage career; sensitive, limited in scope, but patient as the day is long. He eventually went on to teach my students, and at age seventeen was sold to my student, Sylvia Wade. He was lost to colic at age 23, cherished to the end.

Years later, when I was horse-hunting for a young prospect, the seller said to me, "This horse is the right temperature; not too hot, not too cold." I realized this was a clever way for the seller to say that this particular horse was "the right temperature for me." So many riders make the mistake early on of buying themselves a horse that is the "wrong temperature" or simply too young a horse for their skill level. While at the time I did not realize how lucky I was to have my Quarter Horse with the limited gaits and forgiving soul, I understand now; he was the "right temperature."

Even after the experience of training Bodacious, I had a wonderful horse come to me too early in my education. She was and remains, the only horse I ever showed that received a 9 on gaits. She was stunning, and I even once had a judge get out of the box to pet her—she was that beautiful. But, once I got to the collection I lost her cooperation, and did not have the skill or experience to get to "the other side" of the problem. That one did not belong to me and I had to let her go. It still stings a bit to think of her because she never did reach her potential and was sadly lost after she became a brood mare.

Ultimately, we try to do our best by whatever horse we have the privilege to be sitting on. That horse may have limitations, but we do, too.

Learning to develop that horse is part of becoming a dressage rider. One horse does not make a rider, but patiently training that horse will make you a better rider for the next horse. I think if you give yourself fully to the horse you have, knowing (praying?) that there will be others, you cannot go wrong. And anyway, you have a horse. You are not a pedestrian.

It really does "take a village" when it comes to training a horse. While I am not a vet, farrier, equine dentist, or nutritionist, along the way I discovered that should my horse suffer deficiencies in those categories it was MY responsibility. In other words, if it is a horse in your care, the buck stops with you. Riders have to educate themselves enough to recognize good health and soundness. They need to be able to judge body condition. They need to be in charge of vaccinations and worming schedules and recognize signs of a healthy and balanced foot versus an unhealthy or unbalanced foot.

I know some farriers are cringing as they read this. I have never met a farrier that seemed grateful to have a client, with a questioning tone ask them if the boney column appears to be in alignment. Farriers' take a mighty lot of wear and tear on their bodies and sometimes their patience is so strained handling horses, that they might not enjoy giving a tutorial, bent over as they often are with a nail sticking out of their mouth. But, an educated horse owner will ultimately be a better client, and serve the interest of the horse in the end, which is what a farrier has chosen to be their life's work. Still, it doesn't hurt to offer them coffee and maybe even bake some cookies for the extra trouble. Better yet, make sure your horse stands quietly and isn't allowed to nibble on their ears when they go to rasp the hoof when it's up on the stand.

I have also found that it is important to have a vet and a farrier that work well together. Each knows a lot about the other's business when it comes to soundness. If they do not work well together, then the best interest of the horse is not well served. You don't want "triangulation," you want teamwork.

When a horse exhibits a problem of some kind, it is that team that has to work together to help "noodle" things out. Is the horse experiencing difficulties because of discomfort? The old saying "no hoof, no horse" is a golden rule and often where the process of problem solving begins, at least to begin to rule things out.

Along with the vet and the farrier, you need a good saddle fitter. All saddles come from the factory the same left and right. But, like us, no horse is the same left and right, so straight away when you place a new saddle on just about any horse, it will sit crooked. Saddle fitters take tracings and measurement, and use a schooled eye to fit the saddle to both the "static" horse and the horse in all three gaits. (Saddle fitters additionally fit the rider. Riders of different conformation require a different design. The twist, the stirrup bars, and the leg flap can be designed differently on different models and these things can make a huge difference to the comfort and balance of a rider.) While fitting the saddle, it's important to choose a girth that is the right size that helps stabilize the saddle without creating chafing or girth sores.

Bridles and bits too must fit properly, with the size and shape of the mouth, the palate and the tongue taken into consideration. The feeling rider will be able to recognize the feedback by the horse as to comfort and effectiveness. By making sure the horse is not made uncomfortable in the mouth, a lot of problems with the contact can be avoided.

At some point, most of us realize that if we are "in for a penny" we might as well be "in for a pound." At this point you realize you need to know a bit about everything even tangentially related to riding and training. Did I ever really want to know how to drive a tractor and maintain footing? Nope. How about backing up the horse trailer? Braiding the mane? Clipping? Cleaning a sheath (eeeew)? Giving a shot? The list goes on and on. But, let me say that even if you are lucky enough to be able to pay someone else to do all these things, it is a good thing to be able to do them yourself without anxiety.

Most likely there will be a day when you must hook up the trailer all by yourself, and load that horse, all by yourself, and drive that horse, all by yourself, because there isn't another soul around who can do it. In my experience, it feels wonderful to be competent and know you are competent. If you have a full tank of gas and a horse who strolls up the trailer ramp with the rope hanging over its neck, a horse who is relaxed and munching hay contentedly as you pull onto the road, you have earned some honest self-esteem.

Nowadays, there are many more resources available to those who look for them than those faraway days when I was twelve years old. The United Stated Dressage Federation was founded in 1973 (I graduated from high school in 1975.) and it has always had education as its core mission. It's important to become a member and to make use of the opportunities available through that organization. They publish a recommended reading list, publish a monthly magazine, and have on-line teaching materials available online at E-Trak as well as an online "University." The faculties of the Instructor/Trainer and "L" Judge Education programs are a knowledgeable and hardworking group who are dedicated to that mission. These programs are run through a "Group Member Organization" (GMO). These programs are so good that even if you are not preparing to be an Instructor/Trainer or an "L" Graduate they are worth repeated attendance as an auditor, demonstration rider, or volunteer organizer. USDF runs other educational programs, including adult and young rider clinics and national symposiums.

My local GMOs, The Georgia Dressage and Combined Training Association and The Good Horseman® Foundation, have been essential to my development as a rider. I have ridden and/or audited countless clinics and symposiums made possible by the work and sacrifice of their volunteers. I always recommend that newcomers to our area and/or to the sport join these clubs and volunteer to work at club events as a way to join the community and to advance their education and technical skills. I try and give back but I can never fully repay those clubs for all they have provided me. GMOs are the lifeblood of local dressage communities. If you go online to www.USDF.org you can locate your nearest GMO. If you do not have a GMO near you, start one.

The United States Equestrian Federation is our national governing body, regulating and policing our sport (as well as other riding disciplines in America). If you are going to study dressage, the USEF Rule Book is a good place to start. USEF also runs our "High Performance League" for international riders and the "pipeline" of competitions that are meant to nurture and develop horses and riders for international competitions.

Finally, to choose to dedicate yourself full time to riding and teaching is often a thankless path to choose with little hope for financial security. In fact, I rarely advise it. Nothing can sap the joy of riding faster than simple exhaustion and a desperately empty bank account. Riding and training horses also comes with some physical risks (mitigated by good practices and experience). The fact remains that horses can be dangerous. Then again, "repetition is the mother of all learning" and early in the process of becoming proficient, hours in the saddle matter. Making good use of the resources you have, and finding the right balance to gain expertise while avoiding the pitfalls, will be different for each of us.

There are many excellent "Margots" out there. There is truth to the adage, "When the student is ready, the teacher will appear." There are associations and clubs to join, books and videos to read, clinics and symposiums to attend, and hours and hours in the saddle to attain the skills required to achieve whatever level you are capable of achieving, whether you wish to compete or not. Ultimately it is the journey that brings us joy; the horses we come to know, the friends we make along the way, the camaraderie of the shows, the mishaps that make us laugh until we are breathless, the rare days when a special ride is seared into our memory. Wherever you are—start from there. Go.

The Nature of Horses

Horses always know how to be horses. But people have to learn how to be riders and trainers. If you grow up around and on top of horses, you learn the nature of horses without conscious thought, almost in the same way that a child living in a bilingual family grows up with two languages instead of one. I do have sympathy for those who take up riding later in life without this advantage. The later the start, the bigger the handicap. That is not to say that it's impossible to reach a high degree of proficiency without this early exposure, but in my experience, it's much less likely. Regardless, you cannot be a good rider or trainer without understanding the nature of horses.

Horses as "prey" rather than "predator" are "flighty" animals. They have eyes set wide on their skull for a panoramic scan of the environment that picks up movement and anything that appears different or new or out of place. This general "scan-feature" of their field of vision makes sense for a grazing animal. They can relax and eat while still being aware of a large expanse of area. Focusing on a suspicious difference picked up this way requires raising or lowering the head; raising the head for distance, and lowering and sometimes arching the neck to focus on images that are near. Realizing this about vision means that when we keep the head in a steady carriage, not too low or too high, as we ask them to do while ridden, takes a great deal of trust, because we are requiring them to give up the option of changing the neck to change focus.

Even though horses are flight animals, it is a mistake to think that they will not show aggression. I recently watched an interesting video of a wild horse attacking an alligator. When the camera panned back, there behind the attack were a couple of youngsters, most likely weanlings, so I assumed that the aggressive horse was a protective "alpha" mare.

But, it's not just mares; most of us have seen the Hollywood version of stallions fighting. Coltish play is a shadow of the real thing and battles of wild stallions are easy to find online and are impressive. Many of us have seen the photos online that went viral of the mule attacking a mountain lion. They were amazing. Even after the big cat was clearly dead, the mule savaged the carcass. The point being, that a horse (or mule), male or female, will be aggressive if they think the battle is existential. Additionally, when you understand horses, you know that even when a horse is not showing aggression, they can still inflict a great deal of damage simply because they are large powerful animals who can react dramatically and quickly. Even a light "tap" of a shod hoof against a shin bone or an innocent "stomping" at a fly that lands on your foot can be incredibly painful and physically damaging.

As I write in my novel, horses can make many both overt and nuanced facial expressions. Their body postures also speak volumes. They are emotional animals and not sly. Incredibly, I have had people tell me that their lame horse is "faking it." That's preposterous. A horse that doesn't want to work may refuse to be caught or turn their butt to you in the stall, but they do not "pretend" to be lame. Horses are honest. A horse that looks angry is angry; a horse who looks frightened is frightened. They always show us how they feel, sometimes in big ways, and sometimes in subtle ways. Small wrinkles around the nostrils and hooded eyes can say a lot to those who understand, as can the way the horse swishes its tail. To those who understand, a horse standing in the crossties with braced muscles and a raised head is signaling loud and clear.

A posture like that tells the experienced horseman to get that horse unclipped quickly before all hell breaks loose. Meanwhile, the neophyte might miss the distressed posture which required intercession. When I wrote about dealing with spooking horses, I wrote about a time to give a push, a time to wait, a time to reassure, but all those moments can be misread if you do not understand the nature of the horse. Misreading the horse is quite often where people get into trouble.

Horses: Why do we love them so?

This is a hard one to answer fully. Why do we love horses so? Why do we love dogs? Animals do something for human beings that we simply do not get from one another. We do, of course, need people in our lives. But, animals touch the heart in an entirely different way. On the other hand, animals need us, too.

Somewhere back in the mists of time we forged a bond most sacred. It's up to each generation to make good on that promise. Just looking at photos of horses and dogs can elicit strong emotional responses. (I haven't forgotten cats; after all cats were once worshipped as Gods and cats haven't forgotten that! Besides, who can resist a kitten?)

But more satisfying than looking at animals is developing a relationship with one. That sort of bond is personal, quiet, and deep. That sort of bond takes time and comes with commitment. Because true love never did come without trials and tribulations; to get to true love, you have to commit to make it through the other stuff guaranteed to come along as part of the package.

Because we do not ask the horse if they would like to come into our stable (they do not choose who will own them and ride them), we have to earn their respect and ultimately their love. We have to commit to love them before they love us. We must understand and respect their nature, and then we use that very nature to make them our obedient partner, equipped to do as we ask. Somewhere along that process, we notice that they look for us, depend on us, and trust us: Heady stuff.

The attraction to horses seems to be inherent to some females as almost a birthright. I wonder if someday scientists will discover a DNA marker that shows we horse-crazy women came from a specific mother line of horsewomen. Maybe our foremothers were the first ones to tame a wild horse. I allow that the men who also have the "calling" likely have this as-yet-undiscovered DNA marker in their maternal line. But, regardless, I'm betting it all started with a woman. As the weaker of the two sexes, my theory is that it was a woman who figured out how to borrow the muscles of the horse to outmuscle the men. Once she could sit upon the back of a horse, she could say to that caveman with the club: "Just try and catch me now." Of course, men being men, they took one look at the woman on the horse and said, "Hmmmm, forget about that woman, how can we use the horse to wage wars?"

Anyway, that's my story and I'm sticking to it.

Oh, the Mystery of it All

Where I went to college (Sweet Briar College) there were "Tap Clubs." I had never heard of tap clubs before I went to SBC. Some are secret societies, and some are not, some are purely social, and some have a purpose outside of being social. But they all choose their new members by coming in the night and "tapping" on their door. At which point the new recruit is taken somewhere where they are initiated into the group, and in the case of the secret societies they learn special things that they are not allowed to share with "outsiders." I'm only describing the little I know as I was never "tapped."

Which brings me to my point (and I do have one); dressage is oftentimes presented as an almost mystical practice. Because of this promise of "unity" with the horse, and "harmony" and "connection" and other fuzzy words we use in the sport, people can wax poetic displaying varying states of euphoria when describing dressage. This leaves the person struggling to develop a steady contact, or sit the trot, feeling like they just missed that last seat on the bus to nirvana. This language can create the feeling of "insiders" and "outsiders" and also make the vulnerable think finding the right dressage instructor is similar to finding a Guru on the mountain top. It's not like that.

Back to the tap clubs; I once had a student accuse me of deliberately leaving out some critical piece of information that would bring her horse magically "on the bit." I was in her mind, holding back. I kidded her that "yes," when she was deemed "worthy," I and my other friends who belonged to the club of "people whose horse went on the bit" would come in the night, knock on her door, and give her that secret piece of information during her initiation rite. Until then, well, I was sworn to secrecy.

I cracked myself up but I'm not sure my student appreciated my humor because the real answer is, of course, that mastering the skills that can lead to those magical moments is hard; very hard.

When dressage riding is done well, it looks effortless. But, this can be said about almost any highly skilled endeavor. I've had people say, "You make that look so easy" and my honest answer is often, "Yes, it IS easy—now." That "now" might have arrived the day after I had thought it never would. It also may be easy "now" but when I introduce "X" tomorrow it may disappear for a time. I should just take the compliment and keep my mouth shut because I don't want to squash someone's enthusiasm with too large a dose of reality. I think a bit of naiveté at the outset of any endeavor is healthy, gets the process turbocharged but, of course, is destined to burn out. It's best to start any journey full of energy, optimism, and eager anticipation. A bit of childlike wonder helps fuel motivation. You have to be able to recharge that enthusiasm constantly because things are going to get difficult. Disappointment is inevitable, and we all get discouraged.

That naiveté though, once lost, is never regained. It's the price you pay for knowledge and life is really about gaining knowledge along with skill. It's hard when you have been trained to analyze and critique a performance to ever retrieve the total wonder and admiration you had as a novice. But, conversely, when you understand how elusive perfection is, you also are less harsh in your assessments of others. It gets ugly sometimes on the internet when riders who are knowledgeable enough to see and name faults, but not experienced enough to have had themselves put under the public microscope, weigh in with over-the-top criticisms. Everyone, and I mean everyone, can take a really lousy photo that makes them look like a very bad rider. That doesn't mean I am defending abusive riding or training; of course, I am not.

The truth is that there IS magic to be found in dressage riding. We do have those moments that things fall in place and it feels like the "light bulb" turned on and suddenly it's easy. We get into that "flow" state and once you find it, you hang onto it as long as you can. Until you lose it again.

But here's the truth. It isn't to be found by owning the right horse or the right equipment, riding at the right barn with the "right" trainer. All those things are great; don't get me wrong, all horses, equipment, and trainers are NOT equal. But "magic" can't come at all until the rider is ready.

The "magic" doesn't come at one's bidding. It comes when it comes, stealthily and unplanned. And in my experience, it usually comes when there is no one around to witness it. As much as I love the Olympics, for example, I doubt that any rider has their best ride under that sort of scrutiny. But, if you have a chance to watch those same riders and horses another time, warming up perhaps or in their own arena working without knowing they are observed, you may even find them more impressive. While there are sure to be exceptions, at least for myself, the breakthroughs come in moments of quiet concentration.

Once you begin to study dressage in earnest and realize that it is much harder to do than it looks, you begin to feel your own shortcomings and limitations. This is where my aforementioned student found herself and I know she was thinking: "Wait, it shouldn't be this hard!" It's not uncommon to see students at this point make the rounds of all the available instructors in the area in the search for the holy grail of teachers. It's also not uncommon to find students thinking, "Wait, it must be this darn horse!" But, after they own several different horses and eventually find each horse molding into the previous horse, they run up against the realization that "wherever I go, there I am," and the fact that "I have seen the enemy, and it is I." The biggest limiting factor in any rider is himself or herself. And while we are taught from an early age to "not compare ourselves with others," that is what we do every time we go down that centerline by entering a class at a horse show. It can get discouraging.

No one gets those magic moments "free of charge." And if you run up against your own limitations (as we all do), we all should take some consolation by realizing that although we have limitations, we can all gain both knowledge and skill if we are willing to pay the price. Knowledge can be gained through study, and skill can be improved through practice. Both require commitments of time. Both take a great deal of discipline. Why is it that we often think that riding should take less study and discipline than say for example "violin?" Now, I don't expect that a violinist would need the athleticism of a dressage rider, but they would require a great deal of study of technique and long hours of practice to develop skill. How long would one need to study, how much practice would one need to log to be able to competently perform a solo that didn't hurt the ears of an audience? What student of violin would expect "magic" and "artistry" prior to learning to read music and hold the bow properly or pull it across the strings with precision? Horses add another dimension to every practice. No violin I have ever beheld came with its own state of "feelings" or "cooperation."

The truth is that only by paying the hard price of study and practice, of "failing our way to success," do we find magic. That includes constantly bumping up against our own limitations, feeling frustrated, feeling weary in our bodies, and sometimes downright foolish in front of our peers and our "betters." It includes apologizing to our horses who have to put up with our learning curve, captive participants that they are. It means forgiving ourselves for being inadequate, but being brave enough to admit it and keep trying regardless. I have seen riders who sadly couldn't stand to allow the trainer to ride their horse any more because of how "different" (as in better) the horse went for the trainer. Horses, honest as they always are, tell the truth, and riders need to listen with humility.

If a rider is willing to do the study and to do the practice, and are brave and humble, they can still sabotage themselves and their own progress and that of their horse. A rider who carries an intensity of self-absorption or self importance into their ride can spoil their rides, and indeed poison the atmosphere of the entire arena or stable. Some riders seem to carry around their own personal black cloud which can cast an outsized shadow.

Each ride should not be given too much importance, at least until you are riding with your countries flag on your saddle pad. One needs to learn to "make haste slowly." The horse has no ambition, but only knows each day how they feel. And the horse, by nature attuned to small things for their own self-preservation, will sense the rider's mood. A rider's state of mind can ruin a ride before it begins and spoil the relationship between horse and rider.

I remember well holding my tacked-up horse while I chewed out a subcontractor who had made unwelcome advances to my young barn help. I was really angry. My horse stood quietly and listened attentively and then, when I was done, refused to let me mount. When I finally got on he still had his "dukes up." Smart horsy. It was a valuable lesson I have never forgotten.

A productive training session always begins by creating the best emotional state in yourself. There are still plenty of times that I have to "get a grip" and give myself a time-out to get back to that productive mind set, because I know I cannot take my horse's emotional and mental state to a place that I myself cannot go. I also know that if I am distracted and lack focus, that it is totally unfair to demand that the horse be fully focused on me. Once I decide to "take up the reins" I owe that horse as much focus as I expect to receive in return. Part of being a good rider and trainer and teacher is to learn first to command your own emotions and to summon focus and inner calm at will. That is one of the reasons why I often say that dressage study, approached the right way, ought to develop a better person as well as a better rider and trainer.

If you are clever, you find ways to live with the hard parts of riding and training and still find joy in the daily process. Each person needs to discover the small things that make the long days and daily grind bearable and prevent burn out; I call this "finding your bliss."

Some riders steal away for a hand-grazing session or bring special treats. Some enjoy the peace in grooming routines with special lotions and potions for "beauty-parlor" time. Some enjoy riding to music that is soothing and centering. I do all these things, but for me; my greatest joy is simply looking at my horse (especially after beauty-parlor time). I never tire of refreshing myself by long gazes at my beautiful horse, and I am a sucker for a pretty face.

That reminds me of the time I tried a peach of a young horse in Europe, who was a bargain. Boy, he could move, and I tried him in an open field among cows, and he was lovely to ride for such a green bean (he was only three.) But, he had a face only his mother could love. Horses are my "eye-candy" and I need that in my life like an artist needs art and a gardener must have greenery. There is really no mystery there; I had to take a pass. But, that is part of "me" and my "bliss." I'm sure that dynamic young horse found a good home with someone who valued his gaits over the shape of his head.

I know riders who really like to shop for the best and latest riding fashions for themselves and for their horse, and then come to the barn to play "dress up" and at show time they look sharp. I confess I have always been jealous of those who have multiple custom boots in several colors. I say—if you can afford it, bring it on. Take pleasure where you can find it to shore up self-esteem for the bumps in the road that surely lie ahead.

If the ride at the horse show turns out to be a crushing disappointment, you still looked good—and that bystander? The one who used to be you? Well, they are still too naive' to know that your changes were late behind and your horse was too tense: They thought it was magic.

Now they want to take dressage lessons.

A Word about Position

When I went to Sweet Briar I learned many wonderful skills and got to experience entirely new things riding the trusty Sweet Briar school horses. I embraced the entire experience. When I first looked through the class listings for the riding department, it offered exciting options I was eager to try. But before I could sign up for "Cross Country Jumping" I had to take a riding test and a written test to determine whether I could exempt the prerequisite course. I sat down to the written test with some confidence; I was, after all, a prolific reader of riding textbooks.

But, I only had to read a few questions for that confidence to evaporate. It was clear in a matter of moments that I would be taking that 101 class; "Position and Control." Thank goodness, I did!

Ronaldo, Owned by Susanne Miesner, photo courtesy of Selene Scarsi
This is one of my favorite photos of myself becuase my position is never better than it is here. But I cannot take any credit for the horse or his training. In 2010 I was lucky to spend two weeks in Germany on an educational grant from my GMO, the Georgia Dressage and Combined Training Association. I studied with Susanne Miesner and was allowed to take one of my two daily lessons on her personal Grand Prix horse, Ronaldo. Ronaldo was a Bundeschampionat Champion and went on to be a successful Grand Prix horse. It is far easier to look good on such a horse. On that trip a fellow student and I became friends. Photographer Selene Scarsi is a Renaissance woman. By that I mean she is not only multi-talented, but also that she is a professor and author specializing in Medieval and Renaissance literature. Selene's photographs have graced magazines such as *Horse and Hound* and appeared on websites such as *Eurodressage*. Also, I have used her photos to illustrate my training journal because they are beautiful, artistic, and full of feeling.

Position is not a static thing. Almost anyone can "strike a pose" on a stationary horse. Correct position is not simply about pressing oneself into an arbitrary form that was chosen way-back-when and therefore gained the designation "classical."

Attaining a correct position is about finding balance and suppleness on the back of a moving horse. A rider who is not in balance will not have the free use of arms and legs that can move in an independent or coordinated way. A rider who is not in balance will never have relaxation. Relaxation does not mean slackness. It means an absence of negative tension. Balance allows relaxation, and relaxation allows the mastery of technical skills, which builds confidence.

Relaxation and confidence open the pathway to "feel." "Feel" in dressage is a term of art. The word "feel" refers to a rider's awareness as well as the rider's correctly timed reaction to that awareness that eventually rises to the level of instinctual. But, while some riders appear to be born with "feel" it is wrong to think that it cannot be developed. However, I think it is true that feel cannot be developed without achieving those previously mentioned prerequisites of a good position.

Mastering balance and suppleness on the back of a moving horse takes a lot of hours spent in the saddle (or bareback). When in the beginning the balance and suppleness of the rider are not secure, it is the horse who helps the rider in the effort of finding balance. That means a quiet horse that isn't too reactive to mistakes. Even better if the gaits are not difficult or too big, and if the horse is already trained to keep a steady tempo, being "stabilized" in the working gaits. It is very helpful to spend time on the lunge line at this stage, preferable without reins or stirrups. It's hard to convince students to take the time on the lunge, but those who do are soon aware of how "going slow" is the speedier path in the long run. Any insecurity on the part of the rider will block progress through creating negative tension.

I remember well an old-school horse that belonged to one of my employers that we used exclusively for lunge lessons. If a child got off center in the saddle, he would shift his weight to get under them. We never could tighten his girth properly because he was terribly girthy, but it didn't matter as his back was flat as a table-top and the saddle never moved. He trotted and cantered so slowly and mindful of his charge, that I used to say that "Dino" was doing his "impressions of a horse cantering" by bobbing his head up and down in a canter rhythm while his legs hardly moved at all. He gave a lot of riders a safe and relaxed start.

Vaulting is also an excellent way to start riding. When you can stand up on the back of a horse, or keep your balance while doing a shoulder stand, suddenly the sitting trot doesn't seem daunting. Vaulting horses are trained to keep a steady tempo regardless of what is going on up on top of their backs, and so very confidence building. Vaulting horses are trained to carry multiple vaulters at one time. How reassuring to the timid child to have an older kid sitting or standing right behind them?

Vaulting clubs are affordable ways for a child to begin riding since the cost of the horse is spread over many. With multiple children participating with the grooming, bathing, hand-grazing, and keeping the horse fresh with rides off the lunge line, hacking and basic arena work, the horses are treated like royalty. Being a team activity is also a great way to make friends with other horse crazy kids. I wish there were more vaulting clubs available in the U.S. as it is a great foundation for riders of any discipline.

So, what is the perfect position for dressage? The classical lines of a balanced rider who is seated can be described from a side view as a direct line being drawn from shoulder to hip to heel, and from elbow to bit. From behind, the ears of the rider, shoulders and hips should all appear level. The legs of the rider should hang in relaxation, "draped" naturally around the horse without grip. The seat bones of the rider should follow the motion forward when the horse is in motion, but when this is done correctly the action is very subtle. I like to use the example of boats tied to a pier when a motor boat goes by and creates a wake. Some boats follow the wake by lifting up and down "with" the water, and some slap the water by going "against" the wake. Riders all have to learn to go "with" that motion.

The back of the horse moves differently in each gait, but the rider needs to relax and allow the seat to follow "with" the lift and fall of the back muscles while at the same time following "forward" through space. The rider who follows the motion only moves as much as the horse moves them, not adding any pumping or rocking action with the seat.

The torso of the rider should be upright and stable. This stability of the torso is just as important as the following seat. It becomes very clear as a rider gets to the advanced work how the stable torso aids the horse in finding a more advanced and delicate balance. I often illustrate this point by describing a male ballet dancer lifting a ballerina. If the ballerina is firm in her torso (imagine her "pencil-straight") he can lift her and balance her with ease. But, just for a moment, imagine that ballerina letting go of all the positive tension in her torso. The male dancer would likely drop her and possibly injure himself too! A stable torso also has the benefit of creating an elegant rider because an upright and stable torso is simply good posture.

Riders need to become aware of how they carry themselves in daily life and work to keep an "open" front to their torso with lifted sternum. This should not be stiff, but comes from good development of the upper abdominals, making a nice space on the sides from the top of the pelvis to the bottom of the ribcage. The shoulders should still hang relaxed in the sockets.

As the rider becomes more advanced, the following seat and stable torso become the invisible aids that collect or lengthen the strides, making the work look "easy." A seat that resists the forward motion momentarily calls the horse back to collect itself or perhaps to make a downward transition. A seat that releases from that slight resistance and re-follows the stride tells the horse, "Now," to perhaps make a transition forward into a medium or extended gait.

Good position by the rider is what makes the art of dressage possible. It is never a finished product but always being invisibly fine tuned by the accomplished rider in artistic "exploration."

A Word About Control

Control is a beautiful thing. Lack of control is not beautiful at all; in fact, it can be downright terrifying. Just ask anyone who has ridden a bolting horse. A trained horse reacts without thought, as a reflex to the aids of the rider; whereas an untrained horse also reacts without thought, reflexively, to environmental or internal stimuli. To have control of a horse doesn't mean being rough or having a certain bit, it means the opposite. It means you have taken the time to "train" the responses of the horse to the point that the responses are reflexive. As training advances, the "aids" of the rider become smaller. The more control you have, the subtler the aids. To get to this stage of training takes lots of repetition. But, to have the training stick, you can't repeat to the point of boredom or annoyance. It takes skill, it takes time, and it takes consistency. There is nothing mysterious about that.

Submission in dressage is also a beautiful thing and is another "term of art." By submission we do not mean slavish-ness. No groveling. Submission refers to obedience that is willing and relaxed while being instantaneous. A submissive horse does not resist the aids of the rider. When we say that a horse is submissive, it's a positive trait.

The beauty of dressage is that it is a system of training that, when done successfully, produces a horse that is fully under the control of the rider, while at the same time willing and relaxed, giving obedient and instant responses. It's not forced, it's trained.

That doesn't mean that dressage horses don't get frightened or nervous, that dressage horses are always one-hundred percent under control; stuff happens and sometimes we "lose it." But the more trained the horse, the quicker we can bring that horse back to its trained response. That trained response can be a lifesaver, one that just pulled you and your horse back from the brink.

How many times have we been told that horses are "dumb" but then have that same dumb animal make a total fool of us? The horse has wants and desires, and those wants and desires are not always our wants and desires. The horse that learns his own strength learns quickly to have his way if he simply puts a little muscle into it. It's a common problem to have a rider buy a sweet and compliant young horse that has been brought along correctly by a trainer, only to have that sweet and compliant young horse turn into a total spoiled brat monster in short order.

It is a testament to the trainability of horses that a single successful duck-out-of-the arena, balk or pull-off-of-the-lunge-line can be the beginning of established pattern of behavior. How "dumb" is that? A horse understands the theory of escalating negative reinforcement to train a rider without reading a single book. Like children, horses learn quickly how to manipulate a rider who allows themselves to be manipulated. In this regard, there is nothing dumb about horses.

For an example, imagine a horse who doesn't want to leave the stable area to go for a hack. They may start with a balk. The rider may not at this point concede to the wishes of the horse (letting the horse stay home). So, the horse escalates the negative reinforcement. Let's just say the horse begins backing up. Hmmm? The rider does not yet give in to the desire of the horse. But, let's say the rider begins to worry and to doubt themselves. Perhaps they sat passive when they should have been active. Or it can even be that they reacted in a moment they should have sat passive? Or they could have delivered a correction so slight that was more of an annoyance? (The right reaction takes experience.) But, in the end, the horse still has not gotten what it wants, so now it "escalates the negative reinforcement" yet again, this time with a rear and twirl. Now let's say the rider is white as a sheet and ready to concede the point.

Horse now never goes out on a hack. Rider has been "trained." Not too shabby for a "dumb" animal. But a good illustration of why even a sweet and compliant young horse needs a secure, confident, and accomplished rider to train the horse, until the horse has become reliably "submissive."

The amazing thing that I have witnessed multiple times is the intelligence of the horse to read a rider who is accomplished as quickly as reading one who is not as accomplished. The "trainer effect" is real. I have seen a horse change their "expression" and posture the moment a good rider settles into the saddle and takes up the reins. That doesn't mean the rider won't be "tested" by that horse, but I have seen it happen that the "spoiled-brat monster" transforms into an angel before the rider has asked them to move out of the halt. They know.

The "emotional" intelligence of horses is simply astounding. Horses, like children, are happier when they understand and accept the rules. I believe that like children, structure and routine build confidence and trust. There will be days that your ideas won't coincide with what your horse had in mind. But with submission there is a chance of still making things turn back toward the positive for both horse and rider. Submission becomes habit.

Notes on Learning and Teaching

Along my zigging and zagging path, I spent a year at the University of Georgia Graduate School of Education working toward a Masters Degree in English Education. Although I never finished the degree, I did find the classes on learning and teaching fascinating. There is still a lot we need to learn about how the brain works as it learns, but science has provided a great deal of information about learning since Skinner created his box for rats and Pavlov made his dogs drool, although some of the new findings seem contradictory.

Do we simply need 10,000 hours of practice to become masters of a particular skill? Or do we need to take naps and eat well, be playful and make all the mistakes possible while we fail our way to success? While Skinner and Pavlov are still relevant, learning and teaching is so much more than a dry science experiment. It's life in all it's messy glory.

Although horses and riders are not rats or dogs, both think, see, feel, and hear. We are both emotional creatures who are hardwired to recognize danger as well as seek safety. Especially during our formative years, the brain is like a sponge soaking up knowledge. Our young muscles and nerves are nearly plastic as we ask them to adapt to specific exercise patterns.

Our senses are indeed awash in all things equine when we ride. We see our beautiful animal, we feel the horse through the extension of our tack, we smell warm horse and green grass and fresh air, and we ride with the music of the horse's rhythmic gaits and breathing. Additionally, both horses and humans are social animals who need companionship. We not only experience our senses, we feel emotional attachment to our particular animal. No wonder riding is completely addictive.

Learning new things creates real physical changes in our bodies and our brains. Approached the right way, we become someone better for the practice. Teaching and learning are not experienced outside our individual traits and personalities but, instead, rely on them. Whether we are learning something new ourselves or teaching a student or a horse, both experiences impact both student and teacher.

And so, although I do think it is helpful to understand operant conditioning, positive and negative reinforcement and shaping, it is also important to recognize that each rider and each horse is an individual. We teach and train best when we first recognize and then teach toward those differences. Because of those differences, training manuals sometimes fall short. I once asked my instructor why my horse did not react like the description in the riding textbook. My teacher's answer was, "The horse did not read the book." Not only did this make me laugh but, on reflection, it took on a deeper meaning for me.

While we should all read the textbooks if we intend to teach riding and train horses, it is never as simple as it seems in the manuals. This is as true for human students as much as equine students. I remember teaching an adult novice riding student whose schoolmaster horse would not canter for her. The student put her legs in exactly the right places, just as it was described in the book and applied pressure, exactly as it was described in the book. Nothing happened. The horse (although he was securely trained to Prix St. George) had apparently not read the book.

I had to step back from the process and rethink my approach because this particular student was not interested in hearing my analysis. That was not her style of learning. Giving her more information at that point was not helping. Chasing her around with the lunge whip was not the answer either (it would have terrorized her). Instead, I got on and cantered around and made a lot transitions between trot and canter.

In a way, I explained to the horse, almost like a translator, what the rider had been asking in her heavy "beginner rider" accent. And once she got back on he was ready to offer canter to aids that he had previously found unclear. He understood right away and cantered off. The horse seemed relieved, and his expression was, "Oh, is that all she wanted?"

It was a great example of how at that point words were simply inadequate. The instructor (in this case me) acted as in intermediary to translate student aids to instructor aids and then the horse, once he got the "translation" refined her student "accent" into something all three of us understood as a canter aid, because through repetition the rider finally found the timing. All three of us learned something that day.

Each rider brings herself to the lesson. She (or he) has a style of learning. George Morris has said that riders tend to be "over-riders" or "under-riders" which I think has some validity. There is also a scale of empathy. While, of course, empathy is a good quality in a human, some riders can take it too far, being "empathy poisoned" into a state of passivity, which may work fine with a sensitive horse but may be a disaster on a horse who decides to run the show. Too much empathy also leads to heavy guilt every time we ride badly. The horse doesn't need you to feel guilty, cry, or buy it a gift. It just wants to be comfortable and safe. The horse, by the way, doesn't suffer a moment's guilt when it twirls around and loses you somewhere on the trail. He'll meet you back at the stable and wonder why you're so slow catching up.

The other end of the spectrum is the bull-in-a-china-shop rider that is braver than they ought to be. I once had an "over-rider" do something I thought over the top. When I corrected them they replied, "I'm not scared!" My reply was, "You ought to be. I am, and I'm sitting in a chair."

It is up to both the rider and the instructor (and the horse) to be able to communicate to each other in a way that is logical to all three of them and, ultimately, that is effective. While we need our manuals, we need a logical and clear system, great teachers add to that the ability to read a horse and a human and adapt to the style that is effective.

Some riders need lots of information. I am one of them. I need to understand. I want to know the inner workings, heck; part of me wants to be a horse. Years ago, there was a popular book called "The Art of Motorcycle Maintenance." It described two different kinds of motorcycle enthusiasts: one who wanted to get on, turn the key and go, and one who wanted to be able to take the bike apart and put it back together.

When it comes to horses, I am the latter. Not everyone is (even if I think they should be).

A large part of learning to ride is training our muscles and our nerve patterns, and this can only come from the movement of the horse, re-wiring the electrical pathways of the brain through repetition. Which means that time in the saddle where no words are spoken at all by the instructor are still important and necessary. While women especially are famous for multi-tasking and people like me who are by nature "Chatty-Cathys" think we need to be talking all the time to our students, sometimes, the best thing we can do for our students (so hard) is to shut up.

While horses and riders are both emotional and social creatures, horses are not verbal. I have never met a horse like "Mr. Ed" who speaks my language, although I have often fantasized about it. How much easier my job would be if I could sit and have a cup of coffee with my horse and discuss our latest training problem. We could even watch videos on YouTube together. How simple if he could say to me, "Karen, I don't like my latest shoeing job." Or, "I'm sorry you spent all that money on a new saddle, but it hurts my back." Of course, I might not want to hear all the things my horse really wants to say to me, especially about my riding skill.

But, of course, in their own way they speak to us all the time. And if we want them to learn and we seek to gain and keep their cooperation, we have to teach them in a way that makes sense to them. And we have to become sensitive to what they say to us in all the nonverbal ways they have to communicate.

Because they are herd animals, horses do learn by observing. A horse who doesn't know how to use the automatic waterer can learn by watching another horse drink from it. If a horse is afraid of the trailer, it often helps to load another horse first. If the horse that loads first is its best friend, even better. Green horses ridden next to an older and quiet horse generally behave better. Horses are excellent observers.

Of course, observation only gets us so far. We use "habituation" and "desensitization" to start our horses. Horses, to be our partners, have to come into our world. They have to get used to things that are simply not hardwired into their DNA. We confine them in stables, put halters and saddles and bridles with bits on their bodies. We run electric clippers over their bodies and put them in horse trailers and even airplanes. Because of this they have to learn and not be frightened by all of those things. This process of habituation and desensitization should be done gradually and with compassion in a way that does not cause too much stress (although some stress is, of course, part of living and unavoidable.)

Because of this, I do not agree with those who think starting "colts" should be done in a three-day process. Why in the world are we in such a hurry? I watched one such public demonstration, and the horse had liquid diarrhea. Sure, the cowboy was sitting on an untouched mustang in the space of thirty minutes, but I didn't understand what was admirable about that. Why should a strange human (predator) be so quickly on the topside of a horse (a prey animal)? I felt that the human had not earned the privilege in so brief a time. In short, I didn't like it.

But once the horse is habituated and desensitized, regardless of the time we take, we move on to conditioned responses. In the "natural horsemanship" and western riding world these are called cues. I refer to this stage as "installing the aids." For dressage, this is only the beginning and not the end of the real training. Other dressage trainers have often called this stage teaching the ABCs. I go into this more fully later, but a cue is something the trainer does that elicits a specific response.

All horse trainers use conditioned responses à la Pavlov and his drooling dogs after the habituation and desensitizing stage. Remember the dogs heard a bell when they were fed in Pavlov's experiment? After enough repetitions, all they needed to expect food (and commence drooling) was to hear that bell. We do the same (without the drool). We may begin with a whip on the lunge line to teach the horse to obey our voice command, "Trot!" But, once we repeat it enough, like those drooling dogs, we can say, "Trot!" without having to use the whip. We also train the horse to understand (again through Pavlovian principles) that saying, "Good girl," or giving a pat on the neck is a reward. We do this sometimes without even thinking about it. If every time you take a break you say, "Good girl," or pat them on the neck, you have paired those things with the reward of a break.

In training horses, we also use negative conditioning to shape behavior (called operant conditioning). By negative conditioning, I am referring to the release of pressure as the reward. We may put the leg on to "go" but we take the pressure of the leg off when the horse reacts as we wish. Trainers use the phrase "pressure and release" to describe this universal tool of horse training.

Horses have memories like elephants. But, sadly, negative experiences seem to create deeper impressions on the nervous system than positive experiences. This makes evolutionary sense. Some sorts of negative experiences may not be survived twice. Pleasant associations are rarely existential and so not as important to remember. It will need far more repetition and time. But it will build something quite different than that horse I witnessed in the thirty-minute "colt-starting" clinic.

Whenever you study animals in a classroom setting you are told how dangerous it is to ascribe human qualities to horses (or dogs, etc). To a point, of course, this is correct. A horse has a nature that as a prey animal is quite different than ours.

But, I also think that it is a mistake to assume that their minds are somehow empty of only the most primitive sort of thought. As non-verbal animals, they must think in a way that is far different from ours, but, though they will never write a book or worry about the future, they do have thoughts and desires. They have strong preferences, likes and dislikes, friends and enemies. And sometimes they do something that strikes me as astonishing. Much of the time it relates to what they have learned without my intent or intervention. Just recently, I had a large bag of carrots that needed to be used before they went bad. At bed check, I went down the aisle and gave each horse a carrot before turning out the lights. The next night, right before turning out the lights, all six heads popped out over their doors insisting on the same routine. I of course relented—they had trained me in one session!

Occasionally on the web, I'll see a report on "breaking" new research that proves that horses do something that most of us find absolutely ordinary. "They recognize their owners." I can go one better. They recognize the sound of their owner's car's engine. "They remember people they knew years prior." Oh, yeah, not only that they will pound the stall door and whinny at them to draw them over.

I think many horses have a sense of humor. I watched a young stallion, turned loose in an indoor arena to show off his gaits, turn over a molded-plastic, hollow mounting block, stick his head into it, lift his head and then prance around the arena wearing it while we howled with laughter. I've had a foal steal a brush from my kit and play "keep-a-way." I've seen horses in the wash stall work with quiet concentration to get both hind feet in the muck tub. It seemed to me to be the same sort of quiet focus I put into my morning Sudoku puzzle.

What are they thinking? I don't know. I know that although they are mostly silent, there is plenty of things going around in those heads, and that regardless, they are beautiful, charming, and completely enchanting.

A Word About Connection

Dressage riding is connected riding. Connected riding means more than just riding on contact, but it definitely includes contact with the bit. Our bodies make contact with the horse in every place we "touch" the horse. Even though we use saddles, our seat/weight "touches" the horse on its back, our legs touch the horse through our leather-clad boots on its sides, and we extend the reach of our hands all the way to the mouth of the horse through our gloved hands holding leather reins. We use the leather pieces as tools, tool-making creatures that we are. If you begin by thinking about connection in these simple terms, it helps demystify the concept. Starting from here we can then talk about the quality of the connection, and how critical that becomes, because this quality determines the quality of everything else.

When training commences, the horse has to first become familiar with all the strange new equipment and come to accept it. At this stage, great care has to be taken in finding the most comfortable and properly fitting bits, girths, saddles. Because if a horse is uncomfortable, then resistances and evasions begin, starting things off on the wrong foot. Some horses are very sensitive to girthing. Some horses have small mouths, or low palates. Some have thick tongues. All these little things are important.

Poor fitting saddles that pinch, slip, or put the rider in an unbalanced position can turn a free moving happy horse into a balker with diminished quality of gaits. Every rider needs to take time to educate themselves on the equipment we use and how to evaluate fit for our horses. (As a side note, it took me too many years to educate myself on the proper fit of saddles for the horse and for ME. My brain had "overridden" a lot of discomfort I experienced in the saddle. No longer. I need a very specific "twist" to ride in comfort.)

Riders new to dressage get fixated on the position of the horse's neck. And that is understandable. The neck is the part of the spine of the horse that can be easily observed by everyone. It is also the most flexible part of the spine. Horses can bite at a fly that is sitting on a hip bone just by swinging their neck around. If a horse does not accept the contact of the rider's hand, the neck will invert, the under-muscles bulging. For certain, if the neck is not in a good position, the back cannot be in a good position. The neck will tell the story. But the neck is not the whole story. A too round neck with too light a feeling in the hand is actually a much tougher problem to solve, if perhaps not as embarrassing because it's not always obvious to the person standing on the ground.

Once the young horse has been fitted properly with saddle, girth, bridle, and bit and accepts the equipment, then the process proceeds to developing a proper connection from "back to front" where the horse learns to "seek the contact forward and downward" and "fill out the reins in a steady way."

What does "back-to-front" connection to the bit mean? It means that the horse uses not just the neck to make a rounded outline, but that the entire top line is working in a rounded way, with lifted abdominal muscles. This proper way of working creates what we call a "positive tension" and releases "negative tension." The thrust of the hind leg is the "positive" tension and should travel over the long back muscles that run on either side of the spine, through the neck, and out to the bit where the horse is comfortable enough in the mouth to take a steady firm feeling to that bit. That is why the bit must not cause any discomfort as that would discourage this. The rider wants to encourage the horse to "take the hand" and not "hide from the hand." This is important for the future development of a half-halt that goes "through" to the joints of the hind leg instead of simply contracting and compressing the neck.

Negative tension is dissipated through the steady tempo of the gait and properly working top line. Horses that are nervous or tight in their muscles soon dispel that tension if ridden well, and after a time show the release of the negative tension through a tail that bounces in rhythm, a light foam on the lips, and especially a neck that is soft on the bottom side and rounded on the top. The gaits always get better, looser in the joints and springier, as negative tension is dispelled.

To illustrate positive tension in a lesson, often I will hold up a dressage whip and place the knob at the end in the palm of my left hand and place my right hand against the lash end. Without putting some pressure on that lash end, the whip is flat. It is only by pushing the tip end toward the knob end, applying "positive" pressure, that I can make an arched shape out of that whip. Imagine the push of the hind legs like the push I make on the lash end of the whip and the knob end the bit. While it's not a perfect illustration, it helps explain why proper "rounding" begins with the thrust of the hind leg rather than the simply creating a position of the neck with the hands.

Testing Correct Connection—The Stretch Down Exercise

What does it mean that the horse must always "seek the contact forward and downward?" This is considered so important that there is an exercise we must demonstrate in the lower levels at the horse shows to "test" that this is confirmed. This exercise is called the "stretching" exercise. In this exercise, the rider proves that the horse "seeks the contact forward and downward" by softening their hand while riding the working trot on a twenty-meter circle. The horse should follow the release by lowering his head and neck both forward and downward, to the point of the shoulder or a little lower, without showing any loss of balance.

If the rider has created good positive tension into the hand, then a simple softening of that hand elicits the correct response from the horse. A horse who is relaxed and swinging in the back and steady in the hand will most certainly follow the contact in the correct direction. It's important that the horse does not go lower in the neck than it can balance. I get discouraged sometimes when I see judges give high marks to a horse performing this exercise when the horse has clearly lost balance with too low a neck and has fallen on the forehand. There is something referred to as a "gravity drop" where the head and neck DO drop when the rein is released; often like a rock! The quality of the gait tells the truth taken together with the lowering of the head and neck. The gait shouldn't diminish or conversely get much better during the stretch exercise. A gait that diminishes has lost balance; a gait that gets much better is not properly connected in the contact but rather has proven that the contact has constricted the back. Other signs of loss of balance include speeding up or losing the bend and wandering off the line of travel.

This exercise should feel good to the horse and rider and is used by most of us in our daily work as a release and reward at the end of the work out. It is also a way to come back to relaxation after working on difficult exercises.

Testing Correct Connection — Überstreichen

Another test of the correctness of connection to the bit is the momentary giving and retaking of the reins. In German, this is called "*ü*berstreichen" and the German term, though a mouthful is still a shorter way to describe what we do. By releasing and retaking the reins, the rider confirms that the horse is not using the reins as support for their balance (what I refer to as holding onto the ballet barre). While it is thought of as a test of the horse, it's also a great way for riders to test themselves. It's not only horses that use the bit for support or use the bit incorrectly.

By having riders perform the one-rein überstreichen on the inside rein in a bending exercise like shoulder-in or half-pass, riders soon discover if they are pulling or holding the inside rein. If they are, the horse will not remain bending and flexing to the inside during the überstreichen. When riders perform überstreichen on both reins on straight lines, for instance, in medium or extended trot or canter, they affirm that the horse has not been driven out of balance by the rider. (Tip: the ease of the downward transition is also a good test whether the horse has remained balanced on the hindquarters or has fallen onto the forehand.) Although überstreichen has appeared and disappeared in our national dressage tests, it's important to remember that the test of überstreichen was invented to help us ride and train better and it belongs in our day-to-day training regimen.

To perform this test correctly, the rider should not do anything too showy or extravagant that disturbs the horse. The rider should stay upright in the torso and simply take the hand(s) forward by straightening the elbows so that the contact is completely dropped for no more than two or three strides. If the horse is properly connected to the bit it may open the angle of the throatlatch and reach out slightly with the nose as if to seek the missing contact, but it should not speed up or slow down, go above the bit, do a "gravity" drop, curl the face behind the vertical, or hold a neck "set."

Thoughtful riders and trainers get a lot of good information back from the horse by using überstreichen to test themselves and their horse. As "Margot" always says, "The horse is your most important teacher."

A Word About Lightness

We also want the horse to "fill out the reins in a steady way." And yet we hear people wax poetic about "lightness" and "self carriage" with reins as light as "silk threads" which is not to say that lightness is not a goal but it is relative to the state of longitudinal balance. If you think of the feeling in the hand as relating to balance, both longitudinal and lateral, then what you feel in your hand becomes a fluid and relative indicator of balance.

Horses that are more secure in their balance are going to be able to give the rider a lighter feeling in the hand than a horse who is less secure. I don't mind if this lighter feeling comes and goes and if sometimes the feeling gets a little "firm" because I understand that balance is fluid and has to be developed. Some horses, like people, are more gifted in this department. While I don't consider a moment of stronger feel in the hand a "problem" it doesn't mean that the horse should be allowed to use the rider as a "fifth leg." That is something different.

A lot of weird stuff can happen in the blink of the eye with loss of balance. I try to just sit steady in my torso during little mishaps and misunderstandings so that I can bring my horse back to relaxation quickly. While my hand needs to be sympathetic, there is a great deal to be said for a steady and reliable hand that is supported by the stable torso of the rider. The horse who has this stable rider may have "moments" where things go wrong, but they generally come back to "true North" quickly. I like to point out to riders that the side reins we use on the surcingle have rubber donuts to simulate the "give" of the riders closed hand, but I remind students that side reins never unbuckle or change settings should the horse pull on them. Sometimes we need to remind ourselves to be as steady as side reins.

A horse that is losing balance and leaning on the hand simply needs the rider to guide him to a better balance through the exercises of transitions and half-halts as well as lateral exercises that load the hindquarters. At the same time, the rider has to remember to not provide something to lean on or brace against. I might ask a rider who complains that the horse is too heavy in the hand, to do a few walk pirouettes that are small and quick behind, and then ask them to trot out of them. When they do trot out I will ask them to give slightly on the reins and to keep the tension only "the weight of the reins" because for every horse that is seeking a "fifth leg" there is a rider who has been snookered into providing it. Horses that are leaning on the bit, of course are going to have tight necks and as we said earlier, "the neck is the part of the spine we can easily see" so when the horse releases this tension in the neck, the back is also freer and the gaits will swing bigger and better, too.

While riders can get snookered into becoming human "ballet barres" for our developing equine ballerina's, other riders can make the mistake in the other direction, riding around with slack reins thinking their horses are in "self carriage." Actually, their horses are simply not "connected." This horse is usually not demonstrating positive tension from back to front. For that rider, often a picture (or a video session) is worth more than a thousand words. Such a horse will not show a rounded top line with a lifted back and a loaded hind leg, and will generally be moving "on the forehand" with flat and clearly "disconnected" strides.

Building Your Dressage Horse From Scratch (Some Assembly Required)

Horses are born hard-wired to be grazing herd animals who have strong instincts of flight. They have been selectively bred by humans over the millennium to have traits that make them amenable to the process of being trained for our uses. They do not, however, come preinstalled with a saddle on their back and a bit in their mouth or the ability to know what we want from them. Making assumptions about things as simple as cross-tying a horse or loading them into a trailer are sadly too common with disastrous results. Once you interact with a new foal, this becomes crystal clear. They do not understand the simplest of concepts, such as halters, following a pull on a rope, or even the concept of physical barriers like fences and gates!

As owners, riders, and trainers of horses, we have a responsibility to each horse that comes into our care to give that horse the education they need to be useful to someone; to be valuable and wanted. There is so much more awareness these days of the huge problem of animal "cast offs" whose fates are grim. A horse who is an "equine good citizen" is much more likely to find a home where they will be valued. Horses have become more and more expensive to keep, especially in more developed areas of the country. But, a well-trained horse who is sane and sound will be useful and prized by someone; the more highly trained, the more prized. But, all horses should at minimum be able to earn that "good citizen" (imaginary) certification. A horse who is lame, or unsafe, or hurts someone is unlikely to continue to be a drain on someone's cash flow.

Prior to addressing the controls, it's important that all horses can be caught, haltered, led, and tied. They must be able to load calmly onto the trailer. I know this sounds incredibly simple, but it's disconcerting to see how many do not even get a good "pre-school" start in life. Can the horse be groomed, fly-sprayed, clipped? Does the horse pick up the feet and hold them up? Can the horse be showered and bathed without drama?

The controls are elaborated below, but in addition, all horses must learn to leave the stable and go for a hack with company and then alone. (This gets better, of course, the more the horse trusts and is under the control of the rider.) While no one has the resources to be sure ALL horses earn the good-citizen award, all of us who train, teach, or ride can make sure that the horse that comes through OUR hands is given the education he needs for that award. By our handling, we at least can do our best to keep that horse off the "trash heap."

The Starfish story (Author unknown)

While walking along a beach, an elderly gentleman saw someone in the distance leaning down, picking something up and throwing it into the ocean.

As he got closer, he noticed that the figure was that of a young man, picking up starfish one by one and tossing each one gently back into the water.

He came closer still and called out, "Good morning! May I ask what it is that you are doing?"

The young man paused, looked up, and replied, "Throwing starfish into the ocean."

The old man smiled, and said, "I must ask, then, why are you throwing starfish into the ocean?"

To this, the young man replied, "The sun is up and the tide is going out. If I don't throw them in, they'll die."

Upon hearing this, the elderly observer commented, "But, young man, do you not realize that there are miles and miles of beach and there are starfish all along every mile? You can't possibly make a difference!"

The young man listened politely. Then he bent down, picked up another starfish, threw it back into the ocean past the breaking waves and said, *"It made a difference for that one."*

Mandamus, Holsteiner, Owned by Karen Jaffa McGoldrick

Mandamus was my second horse to "build from scratch" having purchased him as a newborn. Here I am riding under the direction of Betsy Steiner at a clinic at my buddy Lynn Leath's beautiful farm in Chapel Hill, North Carolina. Mandamus could be a handful. He was very sensitive to sounds and had to be tranquilized on Fourth of July and New Years Eve to prevent him from injuring himself. Riding him was not for the faint of heart because he never stopped being spooky even as an older gentleman. But he was a dream to sit on as he was comfy and elastic with a soft connection.

Part Two: Speaking a Common Language

Installing the Controls

Horses do not come with controls innate or "preinstalled." That's our job. When we train a dressage horse, we don't "teach" them a lot of different reactions to our "aids" ("aids" is a term of art in the sport of dressage that refers to our use of our legs, reins, weight, and voice, in addition to our whip and spurs.) We first have to "install" a few basic reactions to our aids. We do that by eliciting a reaction to a specific stimulus and then rewarding any "approximate correct reaction" and repeating until it is understood by the horse. Since horses are sensitive to the feeling of a fly on their sides, it is not usually a hard job to get those first reactions that the rider can then begin to shape through rewards. I write more about this later. The rider "shapes" and refines those initial responses in order to develop the horse toward more and more advanced levels of balance, suppleness, and strength. As we develop those attributes, the more difficult exercises become possible.

The rider will install controls that address both the length of the horse, the "longitudinal controls," and the width of the horse, the "lateral controls. But it is not simply one set of controls or the other that make a horse a dream to ride, it is the combining and refining of the longitudinal and lateral controls that make the magic happen. Still, for the purpose of breaking things down into teachable chunks, it helps to think about longitudinal and lateral controls separately and then, once understood, to put the two together.

The Controls: Longitudinal

The longitudinal controls at the most basic level are simply "stop" and "go." They begin to be trained on the ground when you lead your horse. The horse learns to stay at your shoulder, to never pull, and to stop when you stop. Experienced trainers know these simple daily disciplines like leading are critical. We aren't simply "training" when we decide we are training. We are training our horse every time we interact with our horse. It's a good habit to ask oneself each day, "Did I train my horse today, or untrain my horse today?" because it is so easy to become blithely unaware of our impact.

Example: Being a chatty-Cathy myself, if anyone came to the arena while I was riding Bodacious, I would stop and say "hello" and chat for a minute. One day I almost chipped my teeth when Bodacious slammed on the brakes for what I thought was no reason. But, someone had come up to the arena without my noticing, and I had trained him well. He stopped for a chat.

The longitudinal controls in the beginning also ask the horse to speed up and slow down and include backing up, and should include "stand like statue." This immobility becomes very important when mounting and unmounting, as this is a moment when riders are at a disadvantage, so I add this to the mix.

I also include teaching the horse to yield to a soft pressure to the bit in hand, chewing at the bit and following that yielding with the head and neck forward and downward, initially with a reward of a sugar cube. When you do this, notice the flexing response in the poll of the horse, because as well as stretching forward and downward, the horse will also learn later to come back up with that neck and, when they do, they will close the angle in the poll, even as they have opened the angle when they followed the bit downward.

This initial yielding is important so that young horses do not panic at the feeling later of the side reins. Lowering the neck releases the pressure of the bit, and then the horse is conditioned from the start to think of it as a place of reward and relaxation instead of resisting the bit. Of course, it is also imperative to never place the side reins too tight where the horse feels trapped or incapable of using the neck to regain momentary lapses in balance. But, we'll get back to that when we get to further discussions of balance.

The Controls: Lateral

Lateral control refers to the suppleness of the horse left and right (the width of the horse rather than the length), including the ability to turn and follow a curved line without loss of balance.

At the most basic level, these controls too begin in hand. We first teach the sideways driving "leg" with a touch on the side of the horse with the whip at the place where the rider's leg would lie. The horse must step sideways, the inside hind stepping over and in front of the outside hind. An example of when you need this "get-over" control would be when you wanted to move the hindquarters over in the wash stall.

We proceed next to teaching the turn on the forehand in hand with side reins on. This is where the horse first learns to come onto the bit "from inside leg to outside rein" learning about connection to the bit through the lateral controls as well as the previously mentioned "seeking the contact forward and downward."

In this exercise in hand the horse yields both from the inside rein, and the inside "leg" which for now is represented by the whip. As the horse yields to the pressure of the inside rein and whip, the horse moves into the outside rein. Because the horse understands to yield slightly to pressure, he does not resist the feel of that outside rein contact. This "inside leg to outside rein" lesson connects the horse to the bit laterally, and from this lesson the rider has the ability to help the horse find a better balance on all curved lines for the rest of the riding life of the horse. The foundation is now in place to control the shoulders with the outside rein without losing balance and bend. This foundation will support the lessons of the outside rein half-halt, and the use of the outside rein to place the shoulders away from the wall or track and to the inside of the hindquarters in more advanced exercises.

Added to this lesson are the simple lateral flexions of the poll joint that lies right between the ears. The horse can close this joint longitudinally, in the same way we can nod our head "yes." They also can flex the joint side to side, in the same way we would move our heads to say "no." Just as we used a sugar cube to teach the horse to yield forward and downward to a gentle pressure on the bit, riders can check in hand that the horse understands to follow and yield easily left or right. This should elicit a little chewing. Notice with your young horse if the ears of the horse stay level in the lateral flexions, and if the horse "answers" the rein as easily to one side as the other. File this away in your head, because the horse you have on the ground will be the same horse you will later ride.

When horses understand to move forward, to stop and go and make a simple turn on the forehand in hand, then the work on the lunge line can begin. In this phase, the horse learns to be "ridden from the ground" with the trot the primary gait to learn relaxation, contact, and to find a steady tempo. The trot is the gait where the maximum suppleness is possible because trot poses little balancing challenges. Because the trot is not so tiring, the horse can go long enough to begin to fully "let go" of tension and swing over the top line. This "letting go" is not as likely to occur in walk, so best to get to trot as soon as possible.

Once the horse is stabilized in trot and relaxed, its fun to introduce trotting cavelletti on the lunge line, too. Cavelletti not only adds interest and variety for both horse and trainer, they require the horse to use their range of motion without any pressure from the trainer. Sometimes horses seem to discover for themselves new freedom in the stride they didn't know they had; demonstrating how cavaletti are incredibly loosening for the horse. I find that riders who have not felt their horses really swing through the back also benefit from riding over cavaletti. Riding over cavaletti can be eye-opening for riders, teaching them the correct feel of working back muscles.

Riding "from the ground" means that the lunge line and the side reins are standing in for your arms and reins when you ride. Your lunge whip is standing in for your legs. At this stage, the voice commands are also taught. The voice, the side reins and the whip are the bridge that connects the in hand and lunging work logically to the ridden work. If you do your preparation well and thoroughly, when you mount, the horse will already know what you are asking, even as the job of finding his balance under the weight of the rider is new and tiring, and your legs against his sides feels different, the horse will still know what you are asking because he knows your voice commands, he accepts contact, and he understands your whip as a reinforcing aid to the voice. It must be a relief to a young horse to "know" you and your "tools" and your intentions when we, at last, climb aboard.

Once mounted, the process begins of transferring the lessons in-hand and on the lunge line to the lessons under saddle. It sounds incredibly simple. And to be honest, this part IS fairly simple if you don't get into too much of a hurry. However, let's be real: Horses don't read the books. Trainers usually start young horses in the heat of the summer for a reason. That beautiful thing called "control" I wrote about earlier—you don't have it yet. Every horse is an individual with strong and weak points. The horse with the weak back may try to buck you off because your weight is too uncomfortable. One may be girthy. One may be sensitive to sounds, while another loses it over the wind blowing a leaf across the arena. Sensitive, weak horses can start off relaxed and get tenser and tenser as they fatigue, while a strong horse may be full of it at the beginning of a ride and relaxed and feeling satisfied with life at the end of the ride. Since this stage of training is formative for the rest of that horse's life, it is best left to those who are old hands at the process, even though the "what" we are teaching is not very complicated.

Balance, Suppleness and Strength

The "combining and refining" of the longitudinal and lateral controls take the horse from his natural grazing balance which tends to be more on the forehand for almost all his 24 hours on his own, to learning to balance under the weight of the rider. To do this we have to use the restraining/allowing and flexing aids of the reins, and the driving forward or sideways aids of the legs, and the (newly) added influence of the weight aids, to "shape" and strengthen our horse to carry us safely. By safe I refer to both the health and well being of the horse, and the comfort and wear and tear on the rider.

Horses that are "on the forehand" are not comfortable to sit. They tend to use the front legs as neck as "brakes." Those front legs hit the ground hard and stab at the ground when the horse tries to slow down or stop. The "on the forehand" horse tends to work with a dropped and braced back and hocks that trail behind the horse, rather than stepping under the weight of the rider. From the saddle this feels concussive, rough and, in transitions, jarring. I describe this as "going like a wheelbarrow" and if you imagine lifting the handles of a wheelbarrow (the hindquarters) up; pushing it along with the lip of the front closer to the ground (the forehand), then you get the picture pretty clearly.

That's a good reason to rise the trot on the young horse who is still struggling to find their balance or who are bracing the back muscles. Since braced muscles are "hard" to the touch, they cannot swing or absorb motion, but instead feel "deadened." To the rider, it can feel like there is no proper place to sit, and if you try, it's punishing for both horse and rider. Until your horse can relax and swing the top line, and step under themselves properly to carry the rider, it's best to rise to the trot.

Unbalanced horses never can relax properly. Imagine a person walking across a patch of ice. To navigate safely, that person would shorten their stride, tense up their muscles, and perhaps stick their arms out awkwardly, ready to catch themselves. If that person felt themselves begin to slip, they would most likely speed up to try and get across the slick bit as quickly as possible. Horses use the neck rather than arms to balance, but they do all the other things the unbalanced person in my example would do.

Another response to insecure balance is to spread the legs wider. I thought about this one day while riding the tram that runs under the Atlanta Airport. I looked around at my fellow riders who were holding the hand loops that hung from the ceiling. They (and I, too) had spread our legs into wider than normal stances. The tram doesn't make the smoothest stops, and we all swayed over our wide stances at each stop, tensing our legs to resist toppling over our suitcases. When we see a horse that is traveling "wide behind" this is a tip off that they have lost their balance.

It's good to remember that a horse who is bracing the back muscles can likely be a weak horse. This tightening is not necessarily resistance, but a protective response. A defensive holding of muscles though is very fatiguing. After a while, that braced back "gives out" and becomes a sagging back. It's important not to overwork a horse in the initial phases who braces like this since horses who are fatigued are also more likely to injure themselves.

Being "on the forehand" is so hard on both horse and rider, it's important to find a better balance, and strengthen that top line ASAP. It's better at this point to be relentless in a slow way—daily sessions that are short and sweet. Following the rule of "make haste slowly," strong back muscles are not made in a day or a week or a month. Remember that it's always best to stop too soon than too late in any session. Just like starting a program at the gym for out-of-shape people, doing too much too soon can be painful and discouraging, taking all the play and joy out of the process. It's a terrible way to begin a young horse's career as a riding horse.

Longitudinal balance can be thought of like a teeter-totter. At first (and at the warm-up phase of most rides) we are satisfied with finding "equilibrium." Think of the state of equilibrium to be like that of a teeter-totter that has each end equal distance from the ground. If you look at a photo of a horse in trot, and the space between the diagonal pairs of legs is the same, with the hind foot stepping clearly into the print left from the front foot, in all likelihood, that horse is in "equilibrium."

Later on, when the horse has advanced from a "state of equilibrium" to a state of "uphill balance" the space between the hind legs will be closer than the space between the front legs. This happens when the hindquarters take on more carrying power than the forehand and the front legs are less burdened and can therefore show freedom with a greater range of motion.

It's fun to study photos to train the eye to be able to recognize the different states of balance as horses advance in training. It's also good training to study photos to recognize the fault of a horse with too little space between the hind legs and a dropped back with a very high front leg. This fault is called "absolute elevation" and happens when the horse's head and front legs are raised without engaging the entire top line (rather than the correct elevation of the forehand being "relative" to the level of engagement). The tip off of "absolute elevation" in photos is when the cannon bones of the diagonal pair of legs in trot do not come even close to forming parallel lines. Sometimes in this fault the front toes of the horse will flip upward. When seen in motion, the horse in "absolute elevation" while showing flamboyant action in front, doesn't seem to cover much ground because the hind legs do not provide power and thrust to propel the horse forward over the ground.

A horse in equilibrium will generally find comfort in the hand and give the rider a good feeling. Different horses may feel quite different, but for the rider the feeling is that the horse can relax and find a steadiness in both tempo and contact; much like the steadiness of a metronome. Every horse has a tempo that brings out the best possible relaxation and swing. It is up to the rider to discover what it is for each horse. This is first developed on the lunge line where it is easy to see, but it is also easy to feel in the trot. As the horse gains strength, this will change, but it will always change for the better. Many young horses who move beautifully turned loose in the pasture may start out by losing some of their natural freedom, but if the training is correct, the horse will find it again as soon as they find their equilibrium and gain enough strength over the topline.

It may take some horse's time to find this same steady balance and tempo in the canter, as the canter has much tougher balance challenges. When the canter lacks balance, it is also very tiring for the horse. The additional speed of canter can be a source of anxiety for both horse and rider. No one wants to fall down and go "boom." Again, this is where the rider needs both discipline and compassion to chip away daily at the problem in a way that doesn't over tire or frighten the horse. I've ridden some "Baby-Hughies" that struggled initially in canter to the point that I jokingly warned all the other riders in the arena to clear a wide swath for me before attempting canter. But as impossible as it seemed at the beginning, they all did "get it" in time.

For the first couple years of training, equilibrium is our goal in both trot and canter. That doesn't mean we don't welcome those overachievers who are naturally gifted and give us more advanced balance, but for those others, it's enough. Be satisfied.

The walk has no balance challenge at all as three out of the four feet are grounded in all beats of the stride, which makes the walk a great place to review the reactions to all our "aids" in each ride. I like to do a "pre-flight check" on all my horses after I have given them a ten-minute walk on loose reins, and before I ask for trot. This is where I review all the longitudinal and lateral aids, like a mini refresher course before picking up the trot. This "pre-flight" check is especially helpful for horses who tend to be placid or lazy, but be aware that some horses get tense in walk, and some get bored or fretful and want to "get on with it." Be smart and adapt your program to the individual horse to be sure you are not creating problems instead of creating submission.

Developing straightness must be in the mind of the rider right from the start of training the young horse. You can't wait to address it just because it's way up there on the "Training Scale" just under the pinnacle of "collection." For horses, like people, are not naturally straight and in fact are all to a degree born "crooked." It takes a lifetime of correct training to develop and to keep as much even development as we can, knowing full well that the job is never finished.

If you have ever looked down from the hayloft to the horses below in their stalls, you have surely noticed how narrow a horse is in the shoulders compared to the hips. This means that if you ride with your horse's shoulder against the rail, you have made your horse travel with the hips pushed into the arena; crooked.

If the horse drifts into the arena one direction, or clings to the wall one direction, the horse is expressing their crookedness. Just as they do when they counter-flex and fall in on the lunging circle (generally) tracking right, or flex to the inside in and pull out on the lunge line tracking left. All of this should be noted by the trainer as expressions of crookedness.

You might even notice in the field how the horse generally grazes (usually with the left front foot ahead of the right). If you have ever traced your horse's withers for a saddle fitting, you rarely get a perfect mirror image of the left and right side of the withers, and, in fact, the left shoulder is usually larger. For the health and long-term soundness of the horse, all dressage trainers need to focus on helping their horses become as laterally supple and straight as possible. We do this by using our controls and our exercises to step by step make both sides of the horse equal, knowing that we get close, but rarely completely equal.

Because we already know how long it takes to find balance and to make weak muscles strong longitudinally, we have to apply the same logic, and be just as aware and sensitive about the same issues laterally. It doesn't work to over-drill the weak side. Instead, I tell my students to think of a rusty hinge that you oil first and then work back and forth to loosen. I also tell my students to "ice the cake" because, to spread icing smoothly, you gently spread it in all directions. In all cases, fatigue leads to soreness and injuries rather than increased suppleness. Fatigue also creates a situation where the horse will automatically shift to working the stronger muscles, making them stronger still. So, while you are relentlessly disciplined in assembling the bits and pieces that go into a fully trained horse, continue to "make haste slowly" recognizing that "things take time."

It's funny (and helpful) to take a look at your own right bicep muscle (if you are right handed), and then look at your left bicep. Now, look at your left calf muscle and then at your right. Now imagine yourself as a creature on all fours rather than the upright creature you are. In that "horizontal" rather than "vertical" orientation, imagine what would happen if that difference weren't addressed early in your athletic career? Which side would begin to "break down" from overuse? Which arm or leg would likely fatigue first? And since the horse must carry us on his back, I like to imagine carrying around a kid in a backpack. If I were unequally developed, I would keep trying to shift that "load" of a kid over to the stronger side of my back. Playing this "thinking game" is enlightening and creates empathy for our horses.

When I think of that example, it makes clear why so many horses push the saddle (and the rider) over to one side. That backpack analogy comes in handy for a lot of rider position flaws, too. We have to teach the horse to be straight, but as riders we struggle all our lives to be straight, balanced, and quiet loads that move with and not against the horse. I have seen a big heavy man carried by a horse with ease and I have seen a tiny woman create difficulties for a large horse. The large man had made himself an easy load for the horse to carry because he was in perfect balance and followed every motion forward with the horse. The woman had not yet found balance and suppleness and unintentionally interfered. Balance, both laterally and longitudinally, and a supple seat, make all the difference in the world to our horse. And, in return, addressing straightness from the very beginning, through lateral suppleness, makes for a horse who is balanced and relaxed enough to be able to advance through the levels and someday climb to the pinnacle of that Training Scale.

Half-halts

A half-halt is another one of those dressage "terms of art" that can be mysterious and is often shrouded in "fuzzy" language. If you've ever had a dressage lesson, I can pretty much guarantee you've had "half-halt!" shouted at you (along with: "Inside leg to outside rein!"). I've had it yelled at me in a variety of accents and at different decibel levels. But, regardless, lessons are less frustrating and training advances much more quickly when one understands what the heck the instructor wants to see happen when they yell: "Half-halt!"

Here is the USDF definition:

"The half-halt is the hardly visible, almost simultaneous, coordinated action of the seat, the legs and the hand of the rider, with the object of increasing the attention and balance of the horse before the execution of several movements or transitions between gaits or paces."

Got it?

I didn't think so.

Hopefully, I can clarify.

The foundation for all your half-halts was installed when you taught your horse the longitudinal controls, and then the lateral controls and connected the horse to the bit. As you "combine and refine" those controls, advancing the balance and suppleness in the horse, that mysterious thing called a "half-halt" develops right along with the horse.

A "half-halt" is when the rider uses those already "trained" controls we reviewed earlier, combining and refining them to create a better balance as the horse tries to do whatever it is you want the horse to do. It's also a way to "recharge" flagging energy or attention. In the longitudinal controls, it means that "go" and "whoa" put closer and closer together will in time become your longitudinal half-halt.

Shall I repeat that? It means that "go" and "whoa" put closer and closer together will in time become your longitudinal half-halt.

By using the power of anticipation, the horse becomes alert by thinking that maybe a "whoa" is coming soon even as the horse obediently responds to the "go" aid.

Conversely, the horse learns to "wait on the seat" as they "go" because they anticipate the coming request of a "whoa." This bit of anticipation of "go while you whoa" keeps the engine idling instead of cutting off. It also gives a feeling of the horse staying "inflated" under you.

After every "whoa" is more anticipation of "go" because the hind legs are about to "restart" the stride with a fresh push. There is a bit of "go in every whoa, and whoa in every go."

When you see a dressage horse standing in a good halt, immobile but ready to trot off, you can see the "go" is contained in that halt with an eager "desire to go forward" held in readiness. It's there because the rider made a series of effective half-halts into that transition. That good "whoa" started from the driving aids rather than just the stopping aids.

As I stated earlier on the section on position, the torso and the seat of the rider are the reasons that a half-halt can become "hardly visible." Poor positions cannot create effective half-halts.

That other phrase yelled by the instructor of "inside leg to outside rein!" must be understood and reliable in order to make an effective half-halt on the outside rein without losing flexion, bend, and balance. The half-halt on the outside rein controls the step of the front legs (smaller or larger) places the shoulder to increase or decrease in the amount of bend and, in concert with the sideways driving leg can drive either the outside hind or the inside hind leg to take small or big steps sideways, closing up the angles or making them wider. It's all about using those controls you established in your turns-on-the-forehands and then, later, the controls you taught in the turns-on-the-haunches that give you the half-halt on the outside rein.

Examples of Half-halts: Longitudinal and Lateral

While half-halts are ridden in almost every conceivable situation, and can be tiny or bigger as a rider "monitors" the strides, let's start with an easy example of a longitudinal half-halt. Once you have connected your horse over the back and established a steady contact and tempo in trot, what did you do when you wanted to make a transition to walk?

Riders soon realize that if they simply pull back on the reins they disrupt the relaxed swing and steady connection. If they hold ANY kind of sustained backward pressure, the transition will be ugly. The horse may resist the pull by tensing the neck, dropping the back, stabbing the front legs into the ground, or even putting his nose in the air and opening the mouth. Simply pulling backward on the reins can then be established as NOT a half-halt.

Your goal instead is to "land the downward transition like a jet plane lands on the runway, tail down first and nose touching down a moment later, light as a feather." To land this way, the jet plane must keep moving forward, even as the flaps go up to build resistance and lift the nose of the airplane.

Another way I like to describe riding half-halts into a smooth transition is by telling students to "dribble a basketball" smaller and smaller in the bounce until the rider is ready to allow the transition. To dribble a basketball smaller and smaller, there must be a continued push from the hand so the ball will bounce. For the bounce to get smaller it also has to get quicker. For the rider to shift that tiny quick bouncing ball (trot step) into walk, they simply "allow the transition to be completed" by stilling the hand and torso for a moment in the same way a dribbling basketball comes to rest against the ground by putting the palm of the hand down on the ball.

Riders can also be reminded again of the image of the teeter-totter I introduced earlier. In this case, I laughingly remind students to "keep the big kid behind you on the teeter-totter, and the little kid in the seat in front of you." A backward pulling hand does just the opposite. So, instead of initiating the downward transition with the hand, we initiate it with the leg. I know that initially sounds backward. But, let's look at it another way.

We often speak of "connection" as an unbroken circle of energy that begins with the push of the hind legs, travels over the back to the bit, and then returns at the completion of the stride back to the push of the hind leg. By thinking: "Let the circle be unbroken" (or even singing it!), the rider learns how to use the driving and restraining controls to shape the circle without breaking the circle.

Let's be honest, though: it takes time to get to that seamless shifting of balance without any breaks in the circle. When you get it, you get it because your connection is good, your position is good, and you have learned to complete a series of effective half-halts smoothly through tons of repetitions. A gazillion transitions are the gateway to effective half-halts. When they are good they happen "under the rider and not in front of the rider."

In the beginning, this feeling of riding all transitions "uphill" rather than "downhill" takes time to develop. Promptness and accuracy matters more later, but balance and suppleness are what matters most. If the rider focuses on creating that feeling, then they will find their way into a correct half-halt. As the training continues, the rider will refine the longitudinal half-halt. The ratio of how much leg-to-hand is fluid. But, by "playing" around in a happy and nonjudgmental way, the rider can stumble onto a whole new set of gaits. When a horse can shift the weight back and use the top line and the supple joints, the rider may be happily surprised at the new "bounce." This is the place where it gets fun, and it's all due to that mysterious thing called a half-halt.

That's my review of the longitudinal half-halt, but now let's explore the half-halt on the outside rein. Here is a great exercise to play with that illustrates how this works.

If the rider can make an easy forward going leg yield in walk from the long wall to the center line, say tracking right, they will need to use the outside (right) rein to guide the shoulders fairly parallel to the wall along a diagonal line toward center line. This already demonstrates some control with the outside rein as the horse steps away from the rider's left leg, crossing the legs forward and sideways to make the leg yield. (BTW, the term outside rein refers to the rein away from the lateral flexion or bend, not to the orientation of the horse to the rail of the arena.) In this case, the outside rein is the right rein. The horse should be filling up the outside rein in a nice submissive way as he performs the leg yield.

In leg yield the poll should be very slightly flexed to the left away from the direction of movement. As the rider approaches the center line, ask them to perform a half-turn on the forehand away from the same left leg, this half-turn will change the direction. In the half-turn on the forehand, be sure not to allow any stopping of the front legs or lose the inside left flexion of the poll.

How did the rider go from covering ground forward/sideways in leg yield to hardly covering any ground forward as they continued to move sideways in a turn on the forehand? After they made the turn on the forehand how were they able once again to cover ground in longer steps as they rode leg yield back to the track on the diagonal line?

Half-halts! They did it by making half-halts on the outside rein. By slowing and shortening the steps of the outside front leg with the outside rein, and by doing so without pulling on the inside rein, the turn on the forehand was completed. At the same time that the rider shortened and slowed the step of the front leg, they were activating the hind legs, making the horse step sideways with energy. To ride forward back onto the diagonal line to the track, the same outside rein placed the shoulders on a new line and allowed longer steps to go through.

The rider had to apply driving aids, then restraining aids, then relax a moment, and then reapply the driving aids to ride out of the movement on the outside rein.

When I look at this last sentence, it reads like a word salad. But, experiencing the half-halt on the outside rein through an exercise like the one outlined above brings meaning to those words.

When the rider has studied the way the turn on the forehand and leg yields develop the half-halt on the outside rein, then it's time to take it to the next level, which comes with mastering the turn on the haunches, which I will go into further when I review the exercises. By the time the rider has mastered both turn on the forehand, and then turn on the haunches, being able to ride them smaller and bigger and ride in and out of them at will, they understand the technical application of the aids for leg yield, shoulder-in, haunches-in, half-passes and pirouettes, along with the concepts of "in front of the leg" and "connection."

So next time your instructor yells: "Half-halt," and you are working on a straight line, think of a transition forward or back either within or between the gaits, and if you are working on a curved or sideways line, think of how making that same sort of transition with your inside leg to outside rein. That half-halt should be tailored by you to create a better feeling from your horse in balance and suppleness, regardless of the level you are riding.

Vocabulary of Dressage and the Training Scale

Every endeavor uses specialized language. It's important to speak "dressage" if you intend to grasp the finer points of the sport (or understand what the heck the judge meant in their comment on your score sheet.) USDF has done a valiant job trying to standardize the language and the system, which is no small feat in a country this large that has a different equestrian tradition from the European tradition of dressage.

Along with my recommendation to read the USEF rulebook, I recommend reading the "USDF Glossary" to become familiar with the specialized terms. Additionally, all dressage riders need to acquaint themselves with the USDF Training "scale." I'm not sure why it is called a scale, since it is usually drawn out as a pyramid. But whether you are "scaling" a mountain or a pyramid, the idea that it's a straight forward climb upward is slightly misleading. It's still a good guide and a review of concepts for riders and trainers, a check-list so to speak, of desired qualities to be instilled into the horse. The pyramid design does help indicate that progression requires prerequisites. But, each level cannot be developed properly without concurrently developing the others, even if the work in those areas is in an embryonic stage.

Right from the beginning of work, a trainer is assessing and addressing a top of the pyramid or "scale" quality like straightness, even if it is merely on a twenty-meter circle and a turn on the forehand. Also, while working on a top-tier concept like collection or impulsion, the rider is always looking back to affirm that bottom-tier qualities like purity or connection are never compromised. The Training Scale concepts are then both progressive and intermeshed.

The USEF test writers who have designed the levels we show and the tests within the levels put a lot of thought into their creations. They based them on that tried-and-true German Training Scale (Pyramid). The national competition levels are designed to follow the correct progression of training outlined in that Pyramid, and the three "tests" within each of the national levels go from "easy" to "medium" to "hard" to confirm that the purpose of the level has been achieved. The last of the three tests, the hardest, is made challenging enough to check that the horse is prepared to move on to the next level.

Here is a quick review of the Training Scale:

(Pre-Training scale work is the "starting" part of training that comes prior to riding, and about which I already provided "notes.")

Bottom tier: Rhythm—with energy and tempo

Next: Relaxation—with elasticity and suppleness

Next: Connection—acceptance of the bit through acceptance of the aids

Next: Impulsion—increased energy and thrust

Next: Straightness—improved alignment and balance

Tippity-top tier: Collection—increased engagement and lightness of the forehand: "self-carriage."

The published USDF Training Scale also notes that throughout the pyramid the rider is physically and progressively developing the horse and increasing the quality of "throughness" and obedience.

Those of us who are committed to achieving excellence in the sport know that dressage is not simply an athletic endeavor. Although we need to be fit and we need to master position and then master technique, dressage is also an intellectual endeavor. That's why we all need to study. Study leads to understanding, and greater understanding makes for a wiser and speedier training process with fewer mistakes.

If we are talented enough, dressage also becomes an artistic endeavor. Each horse is unique, just as each trainer is unique, and when the two come together in harmony, the sum becomes greater than the parts; we see art in motion. That's why in dressage, you cannot simply change "jockeys'" and expect the same performance. The chemistry will always be different. Now that's magic.

Part Three: Putting it Together

Notes on the Progression of the Exercises

Like the Training Scale, the progression of the exercises is logical (but is not set in stone), and set in writing for riders in competition levels and tests sheets as well as in the Rule Book. The standard progression has been established by the USEF test writing committee, starting at Training level and finishing at Fourth level. Every four years these tests are re-evaluated and changes made in an effort to improve both the tests and the riders and horses performing the tests. (Prix St. Georges, Intermediare, and Grand Prix are likewise re-evaluated and revised every four years, but by the international governing body: the FEI.)

    At the top of each test score sheet there is a statement of "the purpose of the level" that describes what should be confirmed in the training of the horse to meet the standards of that level. In the body of the test, each numbered box describes the movement to be scored. Move your eyes to the right to read further under the heading of "Directives." These directives are there to guide the judge, but riders should pay attention to them, too. I hate to confess how many years I was showing before I actually read the purpose of the level and the directives (too many). To learn the purpose of the level and directives from your score sheet is sort of like closing the barn door after the horse has escaped. Riders should read the purpose and the directives and know them before they pay a professional judge to tell them how far, far, far they still have to go to meet those standards.

Here are some of my notes on the progression and how the exercises build on one another. It helps to also know when to feel free to leave the beaten path without anxiety or guilt; to "ride the horse you are on" and to explore "happy accidents."

After the initial controls are "installed" and tested (basic longitudinal and lateral controls and a steady connection to the bit with working gaits that are in "equilibrium"), it's time to begin to add more "exercises" and slowly "make haste" to develop the finer controls and influence. There is no motivator like progress!

Review of the Exercises

Leg Yielding

Leg yielding teaches the "control of the shoulders with the outside rein" and the "sideways driving leg." This is an incredible tool for suppling the horse, but it is also a critical building block. This exercise flows naturally from the lesson of turn on the forehand.

While turn on the forehand is not a bending or an "engaging" exercise it lays the foundation for those exercises that do bend/engage. The horse would not understand to "stand away" from the inside bending leg at the girth later, unless it was taught to move away (laterally) first in turns on the forehand or leg yields.

If turn on the forehand is successfully "installed," then the horse has learned the concept of yielding from the inside flexing rein and coming "onto the bit" on the outside rein, while stepping away (yielding) from the sideways driving leg.

It's no big deal then to go from the turn on the forehand to simply riding forward out of that exercise by guiding the shoulders onto a diagonal line in a forward going leg yield with that "on the bit" outside-rein connection. At the same time that the rider is guiding the shoulders on that line, they ask in tempo with the sideways driving leg for the horse to move both forward and sideward. If the training is secure, the leg aid should be light. Leg yields can be ridden in walk and trot.

Here is an example: the rider turns down the center line in working trot, and then uses their eyes to sight a diagonal line from center line to a letter on the wall. Keeping the neck balanced in the middle of the withers and the horse slightly flexed away from the direction of movement, the rider guides the shoulders along that diagonal line. At the same time, in rhythm with the trot, the rider applies and releases the sideways driving aid. In the beginning, the crossing can be modest, but ultimately the horse will keep the body almost perfectly parallel to the long side of the arena with legs clearly crossing. The forward thrust of the hind foot as it steps forward and toward the midline of the horse's belly is what creates the springiness of the stride.

The hallmark of a well ridden leg yield in trot is an increase in reach and suspension; a better stride. A stride that decreases in any way is a signal to the rider that the technique is wrong. Leg yields can be ridden "nose to wall" or on any diagonal line in the arena. In the beginning, the angles should be shallow to confirm the proper push of the hind leg and to avoid the evasion of falling sideways too quickly. While leg yields are not considered a collecting exercise and, instead, a suppling exercise, I have found that by playing with my horse in leg yield, I have been able to take the incredible suppling nature of the exercise and really "open up" the stride due to the opening and closing of the legs, and I have created more suspension in the gait through the deeper stepping under the body as the horse pushes off the ground. The "nose to the wall" leg yield is where two of my horses made their first passage steps that quickly were channeled into more traditional collecting exercises. These are the little "happy accidents" that I'll write about more.

When riding leg yield, consider what you are creating for the next level. If the rider is thinking ahead, then the importance of a light and quick reaction to the sideways driving leg holds more value. That quick reaction is going to make your life easier for half-passes, pirouettes, and your canter departs and flying changes. The reaction to that sideways driving leg is going to teach the horse to "stand away" and to "stand up" from the draping "bending leg" that comes in the next lesson as the sideways driving leg moves forward from the "behind the girth position" to "at the girth position" to become the inside bending leg for the shoulder-in. The ability to guide the shoulders in the leg yield exercise along the line of travel that the rider has chosen with their eyes is also of critical value to the next exercise.

Training has to be progressive and logical... and yes, it IS different than riding a "test" to show proficiency or even a finished product at any particular level. In training, we reward approximations and shape the horse toward the ideal. We are often very pleased with something for that horse on that day that a judge would score as marginal.

Shoulder-In

Shoulder-in is "The Alpha and Omega" of dressage training (de la Gueriniere). Shoulder-in is the most valuable of all dressage exercises and one that you will use to some degree every time you "take up the reins." Now that your horse understands to yield to the leg, and has a connection to the outside rein that allows control and placement of the shoulder, you can now move on to the shoulder-in. The exercise of shoulder-in has profound influence on the lateral suppleness (read here: "Riding my crooked horse straight") as well as now taking that horse from a state of equilibrium to a degree of collection. Shoulder-in asks the horse for the first time to begin to "narrow the base behind" and carry.

Raphael Rousseau, Ridden and Owned by Ashley Marascalco, photo by Tyler Hawk | Shoulder-In is the "Alpha and Omega" of dressage training (de la Gueriniere). Its profound effect becomes clear as you advance as a rider. Ashley demonstrates the axiom "My hips with his hips, my shoulders with his shoulders, and my eyes looking along the path of travel." Her body position is enviable.

What are we talking about when we say: "Narrow the base behind?" Earlier, when I was writing about balance, I mentioned how I observed people widening their stance on the tram at the airport so as not to fall over as the tram started and stopped. Horses are oriented horizontally, moving along on four legs instead of our vertical posture on two legs, but it's still a useful analogy and easy enough to witness once you know what to look for, as I discovered even my non-horsy husband learned.

Once when my husband was sitting next to me at a symposium, the demonstration rider crossed the diagonal in a rather flamboyant trot lengthening. My attentive husband leaned over and whispered into my ear, "Wide behind." I had to suppress a laugh. He was right, absolutely 100% right. The fact that he understood the concept and could identify it tickled and surprised me. My armchair expert had been paying attention enough to identify a loss of balance in a trot lengthening by spotting the widened stance of the hind legs. He had not been snookered by height of the front toes of the horse.

While widening the hind legs gives the horse more security, it also means the hind legs are not near the midline where they support the weight of the rider and a lift of the mass of the horse. I was taught to think of the concept of a wide base by considering the shape of a picnic table, which is very stable; six people can sit at it and there will be no danger of it toppling over. However, that wide base also makes it very hard to move around. No talent is required by those sitting at the table to keep it in balance.

Conversely, a unicycle is an example of the extreme end of "narrow at the base." It's very "unstable," yet, if you know how to ride it, "highly mobile."

Now, a horse is not a picnic table or a unicycle, but the analogies are helpful. When you have a horse who has learned to carry his hind legs under his mass by "narrowing the base behind," he IS much easier to maneuver. As the degree of collection and strength improve, it will allow future half passes to become steeper and steeper and your future pirouettes to become smaller and smaller. The Grand Prix zigzags in canter with the flying changes are not possible without this "narrowing of the base behind."

Shoulder-in is the first step and the "forever-after" tool in a trainer's toolbox to address that process.

Here is why: In shoulder-in, the inside hind leg of the horse steps toward the outside fore of the front leg, at the same time, the outside hind leg also should continue to track toward the outside foreleg. Clearly, this places the hind feet of the horse closer together. It also requires the inside hind to step deeply under the mass of the horse to carry the rider, and this deep step toward the mass creates more flexion in all the hind leg joints. In the shoulder-in, the horse "stands away" from the inside "bending" leg of the rider that is placed "at the girth." The shoulders of the horse are placed to the inside of the track with the outside rein while maintaining the inside flexion of the poll and soft yielding to the inside rein.

Shoulder-in, like leg-yield is ridden with the horse flexed away from the direction of movement. In shoulder-in, the horse is looking as if he is preparing to turn a circle instead of looking in the direction of the track he is following.

Although the exercise is about being able to displace the shoulders, it's not really the shoulders that the rider has to focus on while riding shoulder-in. If the earlier exercises were well learned, the shoulder-in is a test for the rider to be able to direct those hind legs to travel close together while stepping precisely forward on a line that the rider has chosen.

The eyes of the rider must look directly on the line of travel of the rider's choosing and the mind of the rider must be on the forward direction of the hind legs, being sure they are stepping actively under the rider. Riders learn this important lesson the moment they take the exercise of shoulder-in onto the centerline without the support of the wall.

Again, the quality of trot is the guide to the rider of the technical correctness of the execution of the exercise. The stride should always feel springier and lighter, and not diminish in quality. If the quality diminishes, go back to the drawing board.

Shoulder-fore is simply the same exercise but ridden in a smaller angle, where the inside hind steps toward the space between the front legs instead of toward the outside fore. It's a bit like "threading the needle." The degree of angle the rider chooses is determined by how far the shoulders are displaced by the rider away from the track. Getting control of the degree of angle and being able to keep it steady is not easy but important to master.

Shoulder-fore is an essential exercise for both trot and canter for straightness. A rider who lets his horse hug the rail with the outside shoulder is always creating crookedness. By displacing the shoulder slightly to the inside and "threading the needle" with the inside hind, the rider creates a horse who is now straight "relative" to the line of travel. If you ride toward a mirror in this slight shoulder-fore position you will not be able to see either hind foot in the mirror. If you ride a proper "three-track" shoulder-in toward the mirror you will be able to see the outside hind foot, but not the inside one. If you ride too much angle and lose the bending, you will see all four hooves in the mirror. In this case, the shoulder-in is lost and the exercise becomes more like a leg-yield.

It's very important in both shoulder-fore and shoulder-in to keep the base of the neck centered between the shoulder blades so that you do not inadvertently unbalance the horse by creating "neck-in" rather than shoulder-in. This fault is usually caused by the rider pulling or holding too much on the inside rein. This mistake is easy to make because a good shoulder-fore and shoulder-in feels less "sideways" than feeling simply gathered and active under the seat of the rider. Riders tend to override with the inside rein when they don't think they are getting enough angle. This is a case where mirrors are an excellent training tool to give us immediate visual feedback. But, feel is the best feedback. Like all the exercises, if the feeling of lift and spring in trot or the gathered jumping quality of the canter improve, you are on the right track. If the feeling of trot flattens or the rhythm of canter deteriorates, then you have strayed.

Counter-Canter

The counter-canter is included in the third test of First level and ridden in a shallow loop that travels from the first letter on a long side to X on centerline and back to the same long side at the last letter before the corner. This is a good exercise to determine if the horse has found enough balance in the canter to be advancing on to Second level. Counter-canter is an excellent exercise to straighten and strengthen and ultimately find collection in the canter because in Second level the horse will need to demonstrate collected canter for the first time.

It's important to approach counter-canter in a way that the horse can be successful and if a horse finds it too difficult and anxiety producing, the rider has to be able to deconstruct the exercise into even easier lines, or simply wait. However, it is just this sort of horse that will eventually benefit the most from the exercise. Riders often make the counter-canter harder than it needs to be in the early stages, by either trying to ride too difficult a line, or by overriding with improper position and technique. The test writers have made this first "test" of the exercise as natural and inviting as possible. But some horses will need to be introduced to an even easier line.

The horse must first be making smooth trot-to-canter transitions, changing leads as it changes directions. Usually the horses get conditioned to take the inside lead because they are used to the wall being on the outside and because it is natural for a horse to turn in the same direction as the leading leg in canter. But in time, horses understand which lead is being asked for from the position of the rider's outside leg combined with the bend and flexion. When first introducing the counter-canter, it helps to focus first on the understanding that the lead asked for no longer is related to the arena wall or the direction around the arena. The horse has to listen to the rider's leg position and the direction of the bending/flexing aids.

An easy way to introduce this idea is to ride the horse out of the corner (let's say from H tracking left) as if the rider wishes to go across the arena on the diagonal, but after a step or two of trot on that diagonal the rider positions the horse right "as if" they are going to turn right, and asks for the right lead canter and then drifts back to the track as soon as the horse picks up the right lead. The rider should canter only on the long sides at first, asking for a transition to trot before the last letter of the long side (in this case it would be K). When this is good, try to hold the counter lead until the middle of the short side, being careful to make the corner shallow. Once that is good, then complete the short end, riding it like half of a twenty-meter circle. Try to come back to trot before the horse is too unbalanced, as this loss of balance is what makes the horse anxious. By the time the horse is making canter from walk, the balance should be good enough to begin to tighten up the lines of travel in counter-canter and to introduce the flying change (if you haven't already done so).

Counter-canter works its magic several ways. Think again how a horse is naturally—narrower in the shoulders than the hips, and how if a horse hugs the wall of the arena in canter with the outside shoulder (let's say, on the right lead, for example), the hips of the horse will automatically be pushed in. Most horses are crooked this way by nature. (Remember how they flexed to the left and fell in tracking right on the lunge line?)

Even after the rider has schooled the horse in shoulder-fore and trained the horse to "stand away" from the inside bending leg, the moment of transition into canter can become a moment of crookedness that becomes an "evasion." This is not "resistance" but simply the horse performing the transitions in the easiest way, in order to comply with the request of the rider. If for example, (now tracking LEFT) the rider rides with the horse's shoulder against the wall, with slight flexion in the poll to the right and slight bending around the "inside leg" (which is the RIGHT leg of the rider) the rider picks up the right lead counter-canter against the wall, the horse has no option but to keep both hind legs under its body. This effectively will have "narrowed" the base behind creating straightness, which is a requirement of collection. It's good to remember that this will tire the weak hind leg.

Rider's will have to feel how far to go and how much to ask to avoid fatigue. Riders should be sure to work both directions equally. The benefits of counter-canter can be felt once the horse has found ease in the exercise. I have noticed that riders who feel this transformation for the first time become "counter-canter proselytizers" as if they are the first persons to ever realize what a useful tool it is. I say that because I was one of them.

On the other hand, a very famous dressage trainer in an interview stated that he never performs counter-canter. I find this hard to square as riding canter transitions from walk-left-lead-walk-right-lead, is a time-tested way to prepare horses for flying changes, and indeed is a good way to explain the tempi changes to a horse, for a line of tempis is simply a line of canter-walk-canter transitions where the walk has been left out, but more on that later.

The half-ten-meter circle in counter-canter used to be part of the Prix St. Georges test many years ago, and was called the "Niggli Squiggle" after the man who designed the test. It wasn't a pretty exercise, but it tested the balance and strength of the horse in a way that was obvious to the judges, and although it is no longer demanded in the PSG it has found its way back into the tests in Fourth Level Test—3.

Finally, riders first learning to ride counter-canter often make the same mistakes. The most usual mistake is to pull the neck of the horse to the inside, which always unbalances the horse, while allowing the outside hind to slide in the turns, sort of like a car would fish-tail sideways on an icy road.

It's important for the rider to always keep the base of the neck of the horse centered between the shoulders. The outside rein provides stability for the horse, guiding the shoulders, so if the horse is tracking left—in right-lead canter, the left rein's job is to keep the neck stabilized. The outside leg of the rider (in this example, the LEFT leg in counter-canter on right lead) must always guard the outside (LEFT) hind leg of the horse and "catch" it—to keep it under the body of the horse should it begin to slide away. The rider must remember to continue to sit RIGHT "into the bend OF THE RIGHT LEAD" even when the bend is on the outside of the direction of the curve. It helps to think on the long, straight lines (going to the LEFT ON THE RIGHT LEAD) to ride in a slight flexion to the right and, as the rider approaches a turn in counter-canter, to ride a bit with the outside leg "as if" they were preparing to ride a half-pass (to the right).

Riders must also continue to sit up and not lean forward or sideways or become too tense in the hip or thigh, because all these rider faults will interfere with the horse finding balance. The feeling of a good counter-canter stride feels very "level" and "upright." If the horse were a car, "all four tires would be equally inflated" or, if they were a table, "all four legs would be exactly the same length." The canter stride begins to feel more "compact" and the "jump" of the canter becomes quicker. The hind legs of the horse can be felt more easily under the seat of the rider.

For horses that find the exercise of counter-canter easy, it is important not to let all the "air go out of the tires" and ride it round and round into the ground. It's always good to test and refresh the gait with transitions within the gait, making counter-canter an excellent exercise to work transitions between the collected and medium or extended canter. As in all the exercises, the quality of the gait should improve. If the canter quality deteriorates, then it's time to go "back to the drawing board."

Flying Change

When to introduce the flying change is something that is not written in stone. While it is not "tested" until USDF Third level test 1 from a collected canter, most horses do not have to be in a collected canter in order to make a clean flying change. It is not unusual to see suckling foals bounding and bouncing around their dams making flying changes. Of course, seeing a horse display his "moves" freely on his own terms is not the same as asking them to do those same moves under the weight of a rider and on the aids of the rider.

It's important, though, to stay open to "happy accidents." A horse's first flying change is sometimes a gift that comes disguised as a mistake. If a horse "offers" a clean flying change without stress, it seems to me bad manners to not accept the "gift" with gratitude. It doesn't mean you skip a level or go crazy by overtraining the changes, but since it is quite natural for some horses, the trainer should keep it light and fun and try to bring the "gift" clearly onto the aids.

Horses who show talent early for the changes generally have good jump in the canter and because of that the mechanics are not a problem. These horses tend to offer the flying change simply to shift over to the inside lead as a matter of convenience and because it's easy for them. When a horse offers one of these "happy accidents" go ahead and pretend "I meant to do that" the first couple of times. Most horses like praise and are happy to take a sugar cube and try to noodle-out what they just did that made the rider so deliriously happy. Repetition is "the mother of all learning" and if you can repeat it, you can train it. Of course, such horses still have to learn to perform the flying change on the aids of the trainer. The trainer should simply design exercises that bring the horse gradually onto the aids.

Here is one example of an exercise for bringing the horse onto the aids for flying change in a logical way. Ride a three-loop serpentine in canter, making a transition to walk (through a few trot steps is just fine at this point) prior to centerline. Make a transition to the new lead on centerline, and repeat the transition to walk and back to canter again on crossing the next centerline. Repeat. After the horse begins to anticipate the transition to walk, only then ask for the flying change. Patterns such as this are only limited by the creativity of the trainer, and keep the lessons interesting and never punitive for the flying change "wonder-child." Be sure not to over train them at first, a good "change each way, each day" is enough at first.

Any exercises that confirms the correct reaction from the aids for the strike off into canter are building blocks for the flying changes. Any exercise that sounded good in your mind but takes you in the wrong direction should just be abandoned without worry. The horse will always give the feedback about what works and what doesn't and the rider should listen.

Not all horses are going to offer up on a silver platter a clean flying change on both leads. The flying change can be a huge stumbling block for many horses. Because the change is "jumped" horses can overcompensate with some amazing variations that are indeed "flying!" Some lethargic types need to "fly" a bit more if it's ever going to happen. The point is that a dressage horse without a clean flying change both directions, on the aids, is forever a lower-level horse—stuck. When you have trained them reliably on both leads, it is cause for relief and celebration.

Flying changes are very different to train than all the other dressage exercises that can be "shaped" over time. They either happen (clean) or they don't. The "shaping," if you can say there is any, happens before you ever ask for the very first change. The real preparation is in creating a quality canter. If the canter rhythm or balance is sketchy, the changes should not yet be attempted. If a horse doesn't react promptly to the aids for the canter depart, and recognize the different aids for the different leads, the changes also should not yet be attempted. If the canter quality feels good and the horse understands the aid for the strike off for each lead, then it happens not through "shaping" like the other exercises, but from a talented rider manipulating the horse into that first good flying change. You cannot train through repetition what you cannot produce.

In all the other exercises, riders can look in the mirror and "see" the shape of the horse and decide if it is meeting the standard of the exercise. They may observe, "Oh, I have the neck pulled in rather than a correct three-track shoulder-in." Then they can make small adjustments of unlocking and letting go of the inside rein while stabilizing the neck with the outside rein, all while looking in the mirror to "see" the result of their efforts. They can step by step use the aids to gradually "reshape" the horse toward the standard.

But, that's not how the flying change is trained since the moment the change must happen comes and goes in the brief moment of suspension after the third beat of the stride. The actual aid to change has to be given a fraction of a moment before the moment of suspension so that the horse has enough "notice" to jump over to the new lead.

A rider must have feel. A rider must have timing. A rider must have balance. A rider must be brave and recognize that moment and "seize it." Riders cannot be wishy-washy or slow in their reactions. A rider who does not yet have these qualities can actually, through repetition, "train" the horse to make the change "late behind." These "trained" poor changes then have to be "untrained" and then "retrained." This process is a tough one and usually could have been avoided. Since "the horse is the most important teacher" a rider will ever have, riders who are green in the changes should let a horse with solidly confirmed changes "teach" them the timing.

If a horse is habitually "late behind," a trainer must first identify the reason. Is the horse properly connected from the hind leg, over the back, and reaching forward downward into the bit? If not, the hind leg can be blocked from swinging forward under the horse properly if the back is tight or dropped. Is the horse moving in relative straightness? A horse who has been allowed to be crooked is often so uneven in strength that the weak hind leg will "trail" or the hind feet will "jump together" because the weak leg cannot get enough thrust to create "airtime." Is the horse still struggling with balance? Is the canter stride too flat? Is the stride too lethargic? Trainers can often feel/see within moments that a canter is not ready for the changes and sometimes need months to focus on improving the underlying problem before "going there" again. Things take time.

There are many approaches to training the flying change. Different trainers have their favorites. Examples include cantering across the diagonal and asking for the change as they approach the wall or corner. Or one can ride counter-canter down the long side of the arena and ask as they approach the corner. One can ride counter-canter on the open side of the twenty-meter circle and ask as they approach the wall. One can make a ten-meter circle at the end of the arena and ask on centerline as they face the middle of the short side. One can ask from a canter half-pass, or ask on the serpentine. Some trainers use a pole or—cavaletti.

To get that first successful change is about "horse manipulation." The trainer has to set the horse up to do something that the trainer can then reward and repeat. The first changes don't have to be pretty. The trainer might have to use strong aids. But if they are clean, they are good enough. Tomorrow is another day—and then there is another day after that one. Make haste slowly.

Because flying changes can be "flying," it's best to do only "one each way, each day" using the exercise that gives predictably successful results with lots of praise. It even helps to do the change in the exact same spot in the arena, and to wait to move it to a new spot until it feels reliable. There will come a day that it feels natural and the horse is eager and knows what is coming and offers the change without any extra theatrics and to a smaller and smaller aid.

It's a great feeling when the rider can sit upright and relaxed on both seat bones and tell the horse "wait, wait, wait—okay—good job!" Then it's time to change it up and take the change elsewhere in the arena or perform it on a different line or through another exercise. Once the aids are understood and the horse can make the single change easily it is time to do multiple changes (at first without a count). The rider then asks for a single change and then after deciding if the horse feels straight and balanced enough, to go ahead and make another.

As in the counter-canter, the rider searches for a feeling of the straightness laterally and for the balance longitudinally, as if "all four tires are equally inflated." If the horse loses either, then correct the problem first before asking for another change. Feel that the horse stays "under the seat" and does not take the rider off either seat bone.

It can be helpful, just as in training counter-canter, to use the wall to correct the "wayward" hind leg that wants to jump to the side instead of jumping straight and forward. A horse that jumps crooked to the left can train the changes along the wall tracking right so the wall does the hard work for the trainer of correcting the left hind. Over time, the left hind will get stronger once it has no way to evade the work.

Eventually though, just as in training the shoulder-in, haunches-in, and half-pass, the rider must be able to "keep the horse between the legs and reins" straight and in front of the driving aids, through all the series changes away from the wall. Once the horse can keep the straightness and the balance, it's time for the rider to be able to put the changes closer together, in the four-tempi and three-tempi counts.

Once the four-tempi and three-tempi counts are holding the balance and connection and are straight along the line of travel, then the fun begins by training the two-tempi and then the one-tempi flying changes. The success of these closer counts is dependent on collection. While the fours and threes can be fudged a bit and ridden in a forward going canter, the twos and especially the ones, well—they can't be fudged.

A horse who makes good two-tempi changes has no time to "regroup" and be corrected in balance. They have to stay balanced. A horse performing two-tempi changes can't fall behind the driving aids and lose power. They have to stay "powered up" and straight. And if those two-tempi changes are to ever become one-tempi changes, the horse has to have quick hind legs that have to learn how to "bounce" from one to the other without "bouncing" themselves right off the hind leg and onto the forehand. The one-tempi changes are an exercise that some horses "take" to like a new gait. These are the specialists. Then there are some horses who "just can't seem to get the hang of it."

At first it is important to ride the twos and ones with a smaller stride that is less likely to lose balance. It is only later, after an exercise is confirmed, that riders can "go deeper into the exercise" and figure out how to make the execution better. First, you have to "get them" and be grateful.

Riders introduce the one-tempi changes through first getting a single "back and forth,"(change, change). Once the horse understands the back and forth, the rider can add one more with a "one-two-three." The exercise proceeds over time, adding another change gradually until the horse gains proficiency. The horse tells the rider how fast they can proceed, and the rider listens, because initially that jump from one hind leg to the other is very tiring.

Some riders also seem to "get it" right away, learning the timing and the count like a new dance step, (cha-cha-cha). And then there are those who have to learn the slow hard way.

Some riders need help to learn the timing of the tempis. I have had some wonderful horses here over the years that once the rider set the rhythm would keep going in that rhythm until the rider stopped. This is especially true in the one-tempis. Reiner Klimke said that the one-tempis are like a new gait. We don't ask a horse to keep cantering by asking every stride—they know to keep cantering.

Changes can be like that: like a dance step—one-two-three, one-two-three, one-two-three — and a good "specialist" is like having a good "lead" as a partner when you dance. A good dance partner can teach a dancer (or rider) to "catch up" and learn the rhythm by taking over and leading (in a good way).

Such horses seem to say: "Hold on, kid, I got this." It happens after some repetition that the rider "catches up" (sometimes breathlessly) to the horse and is thereby "trained." If you have such a horse in your barn, you are blessed.

Riders who are "thinkers" have to learn to stop thinking too much when it comes to the tempis. Trying to "think" your way through the tempis is like tying lead weights on your legs before being asked to sprint. This is especially true when the rider performs one-time changes, as soon as the analytical mind intrudes, the horse will be sure to miss the next change. One-time changes look like the horse is skipping along like a child, and if the rider stops "skipping along" too, then the skipping will stop.

As the changes become confirmed and reliable, the rider can make the leg aids smaller and lighter and sit up and back, and trust the horse. The stillness of the rider helps the horse to remain arrow straight, too. In this case, the half-halt on the outside rein that signals the change goes back and forth like "milking a cow," keeping the time while the rider's legs simply follow the barrel of the horse in rhythm.

While the mechanics of a correct flying change are the same (after the third beat of the stride, in the moment of suspension, the horse changes leads, setting down the new outside hind leg as the first beat of the new stride) the style can be quite individual. Some horses show a great deal of "expression." This is determined by the canter quality, but also by "flair" or enthusiasm. Some horses bring the front leg high or seem to bounce the change; some bring the hind leg higher or bend the hock joints more. That is part of the dance and the art and what makes each horse's performance different and sometimes thrilling and sometimes simply endearing. My Bodacious always grunted with each change and my current horse swings her tail in each change. In both cases, I think it shows how much effort they put into the change.

While the horse that adds flair to the changes is endearing, the rider that adds motion to the changes is distracting. "Manipulating" those first changes with strong aids is one thing, but by the time riders are presenting trained FEI horses hopefully the rider can sit upright and ask for the change without losing contact with the saddle on either seat bone. An old favorite exercise is to put a dollar bill under the seat and retain it through the tempi changes. Lost dollars belong to the instructor!

Turn On the Haunches/Walk Pirouette

I addressed this exercise in book two of *The Dressage Chronicles* at length because for the rider, learning to coordinate the aids and feel what the heck the horse is doing in the turn presents a huge challenge. Mastering the turn on the haunches, while frustrating, is critical as it establishes the foundation for all the advanced lateral work. That includes haunches-in and half-pass and, ultimately, canter pirouettes.

In the novel, Margot puts Lizzy on the "dreaded square" to ride quarter turns to a straight line and back to quarter turns ad nauseam. She lets Lizzy make every variation of error and Lizzy manages to turn herself into a pretzel in her attempts. Lizzy gets overwhelmed by her own incompetence. Then Deb lets Lizzy sit on Regina. But since no horse will do it by themselves Lizzy is still not successful. Deb climbs on behind Lizzy (double bareback) and rides pirouettes in walk and even in canter so that Lizzy can experience the correct feeling. Being able to get the correct "feel" is revelatory for Lizzy. But, even still, Lizzy has miles to go to "own" the skills. I know how that feels!

Most of us don't have a Deb in our life, or a Regina, so we just have to suffer through the learning curve. The important thing is to listen to the horse, and try not to get too frustrated as you take as long as it takes to "get it" since "getting it" is necessary to understand the correct feeling for what comes next in the progression. Later on, I'll talk about "going deeper into the exercises" since even after you basically "get it," the learning process is not over and done with. I guess that's why dressage training is never dull and never finished.

While it's not exciting to noodle things out in the walk, it's at least a gait where you have time to think. To discover the correct coordination and intensity of the aids is like playing the child's hide-and-seek game with a blindfold on; we get "colder, colder, warmer, warmer, burning up" before we find what we are seeking.

What does a turn on the haunches and the more advanced version, pirouette, accomplish for the horse? What does the exercise teach the rider? Here are some notes on the exercise, both on the execution and on the benefits.

The rider begins the preparation for the turn in a shoulder-fore position. That means the horse is bending around the riders "at the girth" inside leg, and is flexed in the poll to the inside, soft in that contact and not held by the inside rein. At the same time, the horse must be connected to the outside rein. This is why the shoulder-in lesson must be secure before moving on to this exercise.

The horse must be active in the walk and accepting preparatory half-halts on the outside rein to shorten and gather the stride (without losing the bend and flexion to the inside). If the horse is not securely "in front of the leg" the exercise will not go well and the more serious mistakes, like stepping backward or "sticking and twisting the joints" of the inside hind, can happen.

When the rider is ready to begin the turn, the rider applies the outside aids to turn the shoulders of the horse around the inside hind foot.

In the beginning, the step of the inside hind can travel more forward, creating a larger sized turn that travels. That's just fine at the beginning. As the rider gets the exercise "show ready," the amount of "travel" is reduced.

The horse should lead slightly with the shoulders throughout the turn, but react quickly to the rider's light application of the outside leg positioned in the "behind the girth" position. It's very important that the rider never be "snookered" by the horse to put too much power in their outside leg. A horse who is slow or dull to the outside leg will create problems for the rider. In that case, riders typically will lean over the leg that is over-working, positioning the rider against the direction of the turn. This makes the horse's job even harder, which makes the rider work even harder, creating a negative spiral of overriding.

The rider must learn to look and sit in the direction of the turn, feeling their inside bending leg draped and relaxed at the girth. I call this "sitting into the bend" and it doesn't mean leaning, but it does have the feeling of sitting upright over the inside leg.

The rider must always keep the horse in front of the leg so they can direct the line of travel and maintain balance in a forward direction. Tipping forward in the saddle, gripping with the legs, and pulling on the inside rein kills impulsion and unbalances the horse to the forehand.

The rider must be able to start and stop the exercise at will. I encourage riders to mix things up at the beginning instead of trying to ride the lines in the tests.

Here are some of the common errors:

As stated, overriding the outside sideways driving leg is a common fault. To fix this, go back to turn on the forehand and get the "step-away" reaction trained to happen from a light leg aid. You can do this along the wall in walk and put the outside leg back and support it with the whip until your horse "gets it."

Another fault is the horse losing the inside flexion and bend and falling through the inside bending aid. Fix this with alternating shoulder-in with quarter turns that are followed by a prompt return to shoulder-in. (Or practice Margot's dreaded square.)

If the turns are not enough forward "thinking," intersperse efforts with walk-trot-walk transitions. Reward a good turn with an energetic free walk across the diagonal, then pick up the reins and do more trot to walk transitions. When the horse feels good, attempt more turns.

So many different things can go wrong, but when the exercise goes right, the horse steps under the body toward the midline with the outside hind, narrowing the base behind. The hind legs are taking small steps that are "loaded" which frees up the forehand. The horse in a good turn seems to inflate in the ribs under your legs and the ears of the horse along with the shoulders come higher. It feels that everything behind the saddle is in positive tension, while everything in front of the saddle relaxes and lightens. In the walk this feeling is subtle.

It helps to have in mind that the horse could strike off in canter if you were to ask. I often intersperse a short session of training walk pirouettes with a free walk to test transitions from collection to extension, from positive tension to relaxation and back again without staying too long in either. I find that the swing and freedom of the walk is improved after creating positive tension in the collection. This makes total sense to me. If my shoulders are tight, I can only find honest release and relaxation by tensing them first. Try this; draw your shoulders up to your ears and tense them as hard as you can. Now let them drop in total relaxation. Feels great, doesn't it? By not staying too long in the collected walk the positive tension never turns negative. By training both back and forth in short session of each I train the expectation of relaxation into my collection, and I train the expectation of activity into my extension.

When you can control the lines enough to practice "the dreaded square" with some accuracy, give yourself a high-five. The ability to maintain the inside bend while getting a prompt reaction to the light use of outside aids, while keeping the horse always in front of the leg is HUGE. Now you can proceed to haunches-in, but first a word about the concurrent development of the longitudinal exercises.

Collected, Medium, Extended Gaits, Plus Rein-Back

At the same time that the rider is progressing through the lateral exercises they are simultaneously advancing the longitudinal exercises. I addressed this already in my notes on the half-halt, but can elaborate. After a horse is working in equilibrium and can keep that balance during transitions between gaits and in lengthening and shortening the stride within gaits, the trainer should gradually step up the demands. It begins with establishing the half-halt on the outside rein on bending lines as previously outlined and also by developing the half-halt on both reins on straight lines.

Riding transitions between trot to walk, and immediately back to trot is a time-tested way to "install" the half-halt. By reducing the number of walk steps between the trot steps the rider tests the obedient reaction to both the driving and restraining aids. With repetition, the horse learns to make the reactions quicker to lighter and lighter aids. Once this is good, the number of steps between gaits can be reduced until finally the rider leaves the walk step out. The rider "aborts the mission" of completing the transition and drives the horse back to trot instead. This becomes the trained "rebalancing half-halt" performed on both reins. With this technique, the driving and restraining aids can be used closer together without resistance or evasion, creating a horse that carries more and more weight on the hindquarters, becoming more uphill in the balance and freer in the forehand. This rebalancing half-halt is employed by the rider any time they feel the horse needs to be rebalanced to the hindquarters or activated or refreshed.

Playing with the driving and restraining aids through the half-halts is where the horse builds strength. The power that is developed can then be either contained or released by the rider. (Remember the lessons on position? Much of this containment is accomplished by nothing more than the good posture of the rider and an invisible aid of the seat.)

Notes on Piaffe

Piaffe is the most compressed and contained expression of power in the trot, and extended trot is the biggest expression of released power in trot. Of course, exercises like the free walk or the stretch-down circle are releases where relaxation is trained as a response in order for the muscles to let go and recover. Both relaxation exercises act as rewards to the horse.

Playing with the rebalancing half-halt creates "happy accidents" where the rider finds a new bounce in the stride. I always tell my students to "groove on the bounce." And by that, I mean, when your horse offers a cadenced step of trot to go with it (as long as it is in no ways backward thinking) and think about how you produced it. Don't try to stay there too long at first though, just praise and enjoy and know that it is there in your back pocket for the future. Finding that bounce is cause for celebration and riders should let the horse know they are happy.

There are many methods of introducing piaffe, but once your horse is working in an active collection and is reliably in front of the leg there is no reason not to touch upon it in a friendly way. The rider should think of piaffe and passage, along with collected, medium, and extended trot as all simply TROT. The guiding principles are that the horse is always being put in a place of progressively improved balance, suppleness and that the horse remains in front of the driving aids, stepping lively, small and more vertical in the collected steps and thrusting longer and more reaching in the medium and extended paces.

Some trainers begin the piaffe steps by simply asking for tiny active trot steps while restraining the forward motion in a careful way that does not clash or block the driving aids. This takes sensitivity and feel from the rider. In the beginning, these are not at all "on the place." This first looks like little "jiggy-jiggy" type steps rather than a finished piaffe. After a step or two the trainer will let the horse walk again or trot out of it. The game goes something like this; "jiggy-jiggy-walk" or "jiggy-jiggy-trot." Riders who can produce a piaffe from this approach are talented and ahead of the game by having the horse already connecting the piaffe to the aids of the rider even though the rider may be using the cluck of a tongue or the tap of the dressage whip initially to support the seat, leg, and hand.

Some trainers begin training the piaffe steps in the driving lines with trot-to-halt-to-trot transitions, using the cluck and the long whip. I have seen masterful demonstrations of this method, but boy, you better be good at managing the driving lines. Once the horse finds the piaffe steps through anticipating the trot off from the halt, the trainer simply keeps them there a moment, halts and praises and rewards the horse with sugar. Once you can produce it, you can repeat it and then train it.

Some trainers begin the piaffe steps "in hand". This method starts with the in-hand whip (even beginning in the wash stall) teaching the horse to lift the hind feet up when touched and/or pointing the whip. It progresses to being able to lift the hind feet up both faster (left, right, left, right) or sometimes higher and holding them up a bit (wait, wait). Sugar cubes make the lessons sweeter! Then the lesson goes to the arena with a helper standing at the head of the horse with sugar cubes.

Crisp halt to walk to halts with the hindleg-lifting exercise performed in the halt are the next lessons in the "in-hand" work. When good transitions can be made from halt to a few steps only of trot and back to halt with the support of the whip, the horse has made a good start. The sessions are always kept short and "approximations" are always rewarded. Any reaction that animates the hind legs is rewarded in the beginning. This is a case where the horse's natural tendency to anticipate works to the benefit of the trainer. After a few repetitions, horses will often offer the "half-steps" in trot in anticipation. When this happens, the trainer stops and rewards the horse (who doesn't yet know what they did, but are happy to be rewarded.)

Whatever system a trainer prefers, the very first diagonal steps are cause for celebration and immediate reward and rest. When there are reliably diagonal steps in hand or in the driving lines, the next step is to sit on the horse and have an experienced helper support with the in-hand whip. That person eventually fades further and further away from the horse and rider until they go away completely. The rider can then carry a dressage whip to aid in producing piaffe, but eventually, the rider has to produce piaffe from the combination of their own driving and restraining aids without any whip or voice aids.

While there are many "roads to Rome" when training piaffe, what counts is that the horse does actually arrive in "Rome." Good Piaffe is marked by clear diagonal pairs, a lowered croup, and a desire to go forward. There are horses who find this exercise very difficult and some who seem to be born with the talent (many of them from the Spanish breeds). The correct feeling is very subtle, but the ability to get into and out of the exercise is a good clue to the correctness of the piaffe and talent of the rider. In those delicate moments of transition, riders exhibit their level of feel and tact.

Gia, ridden and owned by Karen McGoldrick, photo by Tyler Hawk

There are many roads to Rome when it comes to Piaffe. One method is to begin (as we did when we started our young horse) to teach your horse from the ground, then as we did on the longe line, introduce the rider, allowing the ground person (longe line and side reins removed) to fade away until the controls are transferred completely to the rider. Gia is making a very nice start, although here she is still supported by Ashley from the ground. A finished piaffe will have more loading of the hind leg, lowering of the croup and the poll at the highest point. But as the neck is the part of the spine we can clearly see, it pleases me to see relaxation in her neck while actively lifting diagonal pairs.

Notes on Passage

Passage is a very cadenced and powerful trot. Passage is usually only trained after piaffe is well started, and there is a reason for that. Piaffe does not contain the suspension of passage and is more compressed and "seated" and a horse who tries to do "passage on the spot" will soon tire or simply bounce the steps with the croup high, which is a fault. Passage is initially very tiring for the horse. A good passage always maintains the ability to ride a transition forward into a medium or extended trot. Without that "desire to go forward" the horse can become "swimmy" and backward feeling with the hind legs getting progressively "left behind." The way to the passage is found through "driving in" with increased power into an effective half-halt. The progression from producing the first step to a steady rhythmic passage that can be sustained can take time for rider and horse since for most horses building the strength takes time.

Horses are such individuals that many different "styles" of piaffe and passage can meet the standard defined in the USEF Rule Book. This is because, while all good trots are diagonal and regular, horses have different range of motions in their joints and the slightly different ratios of cannon bone to forearms will affect the height of a raised knee. Additionally, hind-leg angles create different movements of hind legs. Some have extra upward snap to the knee or hock; some seem to have extraordinary bounce or reach. This makes every horse express themselves differently in these movements, just like a human dancer or a gymnast may perform the same dance or routine, and yet in their performances produce something quite different in appearance.

My other observation is that I think that in passage, the horse feels what can only be described as a sense of pride that infects the rider. Most horses will demonstrate the passage in the field in moments of excitement or courtship or perceived danger. In nature, horses inflate themselves in passage to appear bigger to possible foes or predators. Because of this, riding passage elicits a feeling of exhilaration for both horse and rider as the horse seems to grow in size.

More Notes on Medium and Extended Gaits

Medium and Extended trot and canter are also exhilarating for both horse and rider. A good medium and extended trot gives the feeling of flying. A horse in good balance lifts up in front and sinks a bit behind and stays comfy in the back, making a place for the rider to sit with ease. A good transition out of a corner onto a diagonal of medium or extended trot feels like "a speedboat in acceleration" where the front of the boat lifts as the back of the boat drops lower. Of course, if things fall apart in a medium or extended trot, the feeling is simply awful. Again, horses' natural range of motion in their gaits affect the look of medium and extended gaits, even as all proper medium and extended trots should be uphill. Extended trots should show the maximum length of frame and maximum length of stride, rather than the medium trots which do not show this maximum. Medium trots demonstrate the power and bounce of passage, but ridden with more stretch in the frame and ground cover. Of course, this is the reason it is called "medium" as it lies between those two other trots.

A medium or extended canter with balance follows the same rules as for trot. Good ones are full of power and lift and eat up the ground in an effortless feeling. If you have a horse who "waits" on the seat in readiness for the transition back to collection, it is especially satisfying to ride because the weight of the reins stays nice and the rider never loses the feeling of control. Again, if the horse loses balance, it will come too much into the hand and be either heavy or resistant in the transition back to collection and the rider will be forced to grip the saddle to anchor themselves until the line is blessedly over and done with.

Raphael Rousseau, Ridden and Owned by Ashley Marascalco, photo by Tyler Hawk | And we have lift-off! It's a great feeling to ride a medium or extended trot or canter where the horse stays in good balance, light in hand, yet waiting on the seat of the rider, ready to come back together in collection.

Notes on the Rein-Back

The rein-back that was started with the young horse "in hand" and on voice commands should progressively develop along with the other longitudinal controls. In the rein-back, the horse steps backward in diagonal pairs (like trot). As the halts become more upright and balanced over the hindquarters, the steps of rein-back become more upright in posture, too.

It's very important that the rider never pull backward on the reins to signal the beginning of the steps, but instead begin the steps backward from the leg aid. When the horse begins to move forward from the leg aid, the restraining aids "block" for a moment. The horse knows already the voice command "back" and will begin to step backward, at which point the legs and reins can relax. If a horse is "in front of the driving aids," they will continue to move backward until told to stop.

It helps to think of the rein-back steps like another "gait," and no rider should have to drive every step of a gait that travels forward. The same should be true of a gait that travels backward. The rider can stop the backward steps by reapplying the driving aids, this time with a relaxed hand and open seat that indicate the way forward is now open to the horse. At first the number of steps backward can be few. Eventually, the rider can play with stopping and starting the rein-back and with counting exact strides back, exact strides forward and, again, a precise number back. This used to be included in the old Grand Prix test and was referred to as "the swing" as the rein-back went back and forth and back (with a proscribed number of steps) and then transitioned to trot.

A good rein-back has no trace of tension or resistance and is performed with a relaxed neck and back and goes straight backward with no deviation of the hindquarters to the side. It should neither rush nor drag in the steps. As mentioned, the quality should continue to improve as the training advances. The exercise is a good test of the overall submission of the horse. The rein-back, performed well, increases the carrying power of the hindquarters. It can become a tool for the rider to use with transitions to improve the balance of trot and canter. At one time the rein-back to canter depart was part of the Prix St. George test.

Rein-back may be a "non-brilliant" movement, but a well performed rein-back speaks volumes about the correctness of the training. If you and your horse can reliably perform a good rein-back, it is a legitimate reason for pride.

Notes on Neck Position

Stretching the neck down is as mentioned earlier a test of the correctness of the training. It is also a release of tension for hard-working muscles and as such is a reward to the horse for their good efforts. But, the rider must also be able to ride the neck back up as easily as they can ride it down. Just like every half-halt, the request for the horse to bring the neck back up begins with the application of the driving aids to "gather" the horse from behind into a now shortened rein. If riders begin the transition incorrectly from front to back, instead of back to front they will create a tight neck, blocking the energy from the hind leg.

Imagine this exercise: Horse and rider performing extended walk across the diagonal. The neck is fully extended and the nose about as low as the point of the shoulder. The horse is swinging along with very long strides and a big overstep. Before the corner, the rider "closes the legs" and in the very next instance quickly and smoothly gathers up the reins, making them short. The walk steps get shorter and are energized again by the rider. The neck shortens some more. The horse becomes shorter in his length.

As the horse and rider go through the first corner and approach the middle of the short side, the strides of walk get even shorter and shorter, showing signs of "positive" tension. The rider then asks for a few piaffe steps. The horse is very gathered, the neck is up and arched and the hind legs hold positive tension as they make tiny trot steps. Then imagine as they go back to collected walk they approach the next corner and turn back onto the diagonal. This time the rider once again applies the driving aids, but this time, as the horse reaches to the bit, the rider lets the reins slip through her fingers and the horse follows the "give" forward and down and, once again, they perform extended walk across the arena on long reins, neck stretched out and down. It's a nice image and not as easy as it sounds, but a worthy goal.

This ability to compress and raise the neck to "gather" the horse for work has to be instilled along with the half-halts. The horse doesn't need to know how to piaffe before the rider practices the "idea" of the exercise outlined above. The simple exercise from Training level of a free walk across the diagonal to a "gathering" for a transition to working trot is where the lesson begins. Riders need to understand that, eventually, the activating of the hindquarters in that "gathering" is someday going to need to be good enough to ask for piaffe or passage after that diagonal. With this is mind at the beginning, the correct foundation is being laid.

Notes on Haunches-In (Travers), Haunches-Out (Renvers) and Half-Pass

Once the horse and rider can execute a turn on the haunches/walk pirouette, they are ready to perform haunches-in. It's best to start the haunches in on the wall where there is plenty of support to keep the line of travel clear for both horse and rider. Later, different orientations and lines of travel increase the level of difficulty. Added to that are challenging variations (counter change of hand and those darn zigzags in canter!) The rider can first sort out the aids in walk, insisting on the horse's quick reactions to light aids. But then, as always, the trot is the gait to confirm the exercise, and the canter is added only when the trot exercise is stabilized.

While shoulder-in is the "Alpha and Omega" of dressage training, the haunches-in feels transformative. Riding those first lofty trot half-passes feels like getting your "official Dressage Rider Club" membership card. That's not to say a rider's first efforts will qualify for that card! Riders can contort themselves, leaning over the outside leg and overriding the exercise. Often, first efforts include driving the quarters ahead of the shoulders which turns what usually is an elegant exercise into the look of a crab scuttling sideways across the arena. The key feedback for riders from the horse is always the same; the quality of the stride should always feel improved rather than decreased by the exercise. If the "tires go flat" then back to the drawing board you go.

When riders begin along the wall, it is helpful to either have a mirror or a ground person to help. If, like in the turn on the haunches, the rider prepares with the shoulder-fore, they confirm the inside flexion and bend and are more likely to sit correctly "inside the bend" with their weight aids *with* instead of against the bend.

Once that shoulder-fore is established, the rider then maintains the slightly inward position of the shoulders with the outside rein as they use the outside, sideways-driving leg to ask the horse to quickly "step away" and displace the quarters to the inside. In the mirror, the rider should confirm that the horse continues to step straight ahead with the front hooves always "pointing the toes and ears" along the line of travel.

While the exercise, when done correctly along the wall, should show four tracks in the mirror, it is the control of the shoulders rather than the amount of sideways step which is the first critical point of the lesson for riders. The honest bend and engagement of haunches-in comes from the ability of the outside rein to control the exact placement of the shoulders as much as the sideways reaction from the outside leg. The exercise should not begin until the shoulders (and ears) are well positioned or, as I have been told: "Aim first before you shoot."

This part of the lesson becomes clear to the rider as soon as they must ride the exercise away from the support of the wall, either on center line, quarter lines, or on diagonal lines. Haunches-in (or haunches-out or half-pass) correctly ridden depends on the rider focusing on and placing the shoulders as much on the outside hind leg. Hopefully, this lesson is well learned in the turn on the haunches/walk pirouette and is able to be carried over smoothly.

The exercise often goes by the French names, and this nonstandardization of terminology can confuse students. The name of our sport is French, "dressage" being a French word for training. In the old texts, a trainer would be said to "dress" a horse. The exercise of "tail to the inside" was called "travers" and "tail to the wall was called "renvers." (I just realized that saying "tail to the inside/outside" adds a third way to describe this exercise!) Trainers often interchange the French and English terms and riders need to familiarize themselves with the different names.

We don't really teach the horse a lot of different controls and the exercises of travers and renvers and half-pass are not different exercises (as far as the aids, or the effect that the aids are producing). The different names refer more to the orientation of the horse to the arena or the lines of travel chosen. (By the way, in the old texts the arena is called the "manege.") But, that doesn't mean that the different lines or orientations don't create different challenges; they do. The haunches-in movements that are asked in an USDF Second level test in trot are nothing like the trot half-passes in the FEI Grand Prix test in difficulty or engagement. The canter half-passes asked for in an USEF Third level test bear little resemblance to the incredibly difficult Grand Prix zigzag.

Notes on Counter Change of Hand/Zigzags in Half-Pass

Since engagement of the hindquarters increases lightness of the shoulders and hence maneuverability, horses that attain collection can change flexion and bend and direction with increasing facility. The more advanced the degree of collection, the steeper the half-pass lines can be ridden, and the quicker the rider can switch from one direction to the other.

Counter change of hand seems an odd way to describe the exercise. In the old days, the direction of travel was called "hand." So, for example, a trainer might say, make a "left-hand turn" at C. (Today we say: "Track left.") So, to make a "change of hand" means to change direction. To change from one direction to the other is to head off in the "counter" direction, hence the clumsy name of "Counter Change of Hand." Zigzag is a common expression for the same exercise that clearly brings to mind the line of travel that is ridden in the half-passes. The exercise of zigzags can be ridden in both trot and canter with numbers of strides decreased and steepness of line (degree of bending) increased to up the level of difficulty. To make zigzags in canter increases the challenge by adding the flying change.

The correct riding of the zigzag requires more than a high degree of collection; it requires a lot of technical skill from the rider. Since the shoulders of the horse are narrower than the hips, riders that don't place the shoulder correctly in shoulder-fore to the new direction (quickly!) prior to beginning the new half-pass will immediately feel the movement deteriorate. Riders also have to be sure that the flying change itself doesn't slide or get crooked. This is one exercise that even the kindest of horses can't do the technical "set up" and cover for the inexperienced rider. (At least, I haven't yet sat on this wonder horse.)

Riders learn the technical skill first by learning to prepare the horse for a proper half-pass. Then to add the difficulty of the counter change of hand they have to break things down to learn the set up to zig and then zag. It helps to make the counter-change on easy lines before they begin to tighten things up.

The earliest attempts can be ridden down the long sides with counted strides, taking as much time as needed to straighten the horse out of the half-pass, establish flexion and bend in the new direction before half-passing back to the track. Once the technique is confirmed at walk and trot, then the canter with the additional problem of setting up for the flying change can be attempted. Flying changes have to be prepared by finishing the last step of half-pass with a touch of "haunches leading" in order to be already positioned in shoulder-fore position for the new direction. The flying change itself must be arrow straight before the horse is allowed to step sideways into the new half-pass. It's best while learning zigzags to ride a few extra strides to confirm the preparation was correct so that horses do not get behind the driving aids, throw themselves sideways, or in any way "take over."

When the exercise has been "noodled-out" with the support of the wall, the exercise can be attempted from center line. This adds a lot of difficulty. It helps to have mirrors so the rider can see the positioning of the horse. Mistakes are normal and part of the process. If the collection is not up to the level, it will soon become apparent and that's good information, too. Sometimes figuring out how to coordinate the aids has to go through a steep "learning curve." Sometimes it helps to add traffic cones for visual guides. It helps to have that tool box "wide and deep" so if riders get frustrated, they can try another approach. Things take time. Be patient. It's also good to remember to laugh.

Notes on the Halt

Landing a square and immobile halt feels great and it looks great, too. A square halt is the product of a well prepared and balanced transition. When the horse gathers itself in preparation for the halt, it's more likely to "land" the halt square with "a leg in each corner" and hind legs "well engaged" beneath the center of mass. A good halt is more likely to step off in an uphill balance and straight when the rider asks the horse to trot on.

Some horses, by nature, seem to adjust themselves into a good square halt. If you have such a horse; lucky you. Most horses and riders have to train a square and balanced halt through improved preparation and execution. Once a horse has learned the balance from trot to a square halt, they have to relearn the more difficult transition from canter to halt. As the horse and rider progress through the levels of training, the odds should improve that the rider will land that desirable square halt.

Horses are more likely to land square in the front legs, but often leave a hind leg "trailing." If you teach a horse to "square up" the hind legs in hand, then it's not such a hard thing to transfer that trained reaction of bringing up the trailing hind leg with a small nudge of a spur on the side of the trailing leg. But riders have to ask almost before the halt is completed in order to train the horse to "develop the habit" of squaring up the halt. It helps to have a mirror or a ground person so the rider does not "untrain" immobility in the process of training a horse to "finish" the square halt. Riders can fiddle around too much and spoil the immobility. Horses who have been trained to "stand like statue" are now confused and "untrained" and become fidgety. Again, riders need to ask themselves the hard question, "Am I training my horse, or untraining my horse?"

If a horse lands a halt with a front leg left behind it's always the fault of the rider who stopped a front leg with a rein before the horse had completed the halt. The good news is that riders can feel this and see it, too. In that case, simply close the leg, soften the corresponding rein, and allow the horse to finish the halt in front.

A horse can also land a square halt that is too deeply under with the hind legs for the horse to be able to make a transition forward out of it. It's still the fault of the rider who has driven the hind legs too far under. To get out of trouble, the rider will need to allow the horse to take a step out of the halt in walk before it can possibly make a forward transition. If the rider doesn't allow the step of walk, the horse could end up having to "break out" of the stressful stance by doing something that belongs in the Spanish Riding School as in "airs above the ground." These moves rarely impress the judges, at least not in a good way.

Rider/Owner Ashley Marascalco, photo by Tyler Hawk
Canter pirouettes take a great deal of strength and balance. I love how in this photo, even though Raphael is performing a real test of strength, his ears are relaxed and hanging to the sides. Ashley is correctly sitting "into the bend." Raphael is correctly filling out the outside rein, which is turning his shoulders around the inside hind leg. He does this without losing the bend around that inside leg. Ashley's upright and stable torso helps her horse maintain his balance in this difficult exercise.

Canter Pirouettes

Canter pirouettes represent the highest level of collection in canter. In order to be able to perform pirouettes in canter, the horse must have developed a high degree of carrying power in the hindquarters and be fairly advanced in their training. While all the controls were installed in the walk pirouettes and then confirmed and strengthened in the collected trot work, it's still a huge step to be able to take those lessons into the canter. As in everything else, deficiencies in the basic training will make themselves apparent when the rider steps up the demands.

While some horses have a talent for the canter work, most will have to build the strength and find the balance over time and will fatigue more quickly in canter than they do in trot. Because of this, the work done prior to ever trying to turn a pirouette is the required "donkey work" that has to be done to be able to get to the fun stuff. Riders may need to give the horse more small breaks and mix in other work to be sure they build rather than wear down the muscles.

Once you get to the point of fatigue, compliant horses will develop "evasions" in order to do as they are asked and less compliant horses will sometimes find impressive ways to resist. Better always to stop too soon, rather than too late. On the other hand, the only way muscles get stronger is to stress them a little bit. It takes wisdom and experience to figure out where the line should be drawn.

While everything on the training scale is important in the building of a canter pirouette, it is especially critical that the horse "stay in front of the leg." It's impossible for riders to retain control of the line of travel and the balance if the horse drops behind the aids. It's also fairly common to see this mistake happen and goes to the heart of what collection is and isn't. The way the USEF tests are written are a helpful guide to "test" that this "in front of the leg" quality is maintained before the actual turns are attempted.

In Fourth Level Test 1, the rider has to show five or six strides of "very collected canter" and then be able to ride back out of those strides. In Fourth Level Test 2, the horse and rider have to ride just a few steps of turn and then be able to again ride out of it (From the test: H to X, and a turn to the line from X out of the pirouette steps back toward M).

By Fourth Level Test 3, the rider performs a half "working pirouette" that is allowed to travel forward three meters.

The training of canter pirouettes begins with the canter/walk/canter transitions. Especially in the downward transition from canter to walk, the horse must not perform the transition before the rider allows it. The rider must always retain the option of not completing the transition but instead "aborting the mission" and riding forward again in canter. Since repetition is "the mother of all learning," horses are not being "bad" when they give the rider the answer before the question can be fully asked, they are often just the opposite, eager to go ahead and do what they are certain is just about to be asked.

Trainers use the power of anticipation all the time in order to train the horse, and while anticipation can work for the trainer (say in the beginning where you ask the horse to pick up the canter in the same spot in the arena) it can work against the trainer, too. By "playing" with the horse in the transitions the rider develops and tests the "desire to go forward," making sure that desire is always strictly maintained.

Sometimes the horse is a bit surprised at what the rider had in mind. Better to laugh and appreciate the "try" and encourage the horse with some forward going canter. This "game" also helps create in the horse a hind leg that is quick and retains "positive" tension. This positive tension was mentioned prior in this text when discussing other movements such as halt. The horse needs to be trained that they can't "let go" of the positive muscle tension when they finally are allowed to complete the transition to walk. Retaining positive tension means when the trainer decides to allow the transition to be completed to the walk, the horse has to hold enough tension in the muscles to be able to strike off again into canter.

At the beginning, however, riders have to take care not to stay in that "very collected" step too long to prevent the "overloading" of the hind leg. If the hind leg "overloads," the horse simply cannot go forward in canter but instead gets "stuck." This is a signal to the rider to ask for fewer steps or steps that are not so much "on the place."

Once the rider can make those canter/walk/canter transitions they can try to make more of those "very collected" canter steps. These types of steps are also called "school canter" or "pirouette canter." It helps to think of the tempo of the canter stride getting quicker in these steps instead of slower. Since the actual suspension time is reduced, this is mechanically true. But, at the same time, each horse has a distinctive way of moving that gives expression to the collected canter steps.

While all horses will lighten the forehand as they take more weight behind (this is what makes the small turn possible) all horses will have a tempo where they look the best and perform with more ease. This can change, too, as the horse gains strength and balance. Trainers, as always, have the job to "shape" and "reward approximations" so that the horse never gets discouraged but continues to develop in a positive way.

It's only when the horse can take very collected steps, keep the rhythm and ride forward out of the collection that the rider adds the turning. But, of course, the turn is not new for the horse. By this time both horse and rider can perform small and active walk pirouettes. The pirouettes can also be made in very small trot steps. The process of taking that trained turning into the canter work is gradual but should still be logical to the horse.

So, for example, the rider can "ride the square," testing the ability to ride forward after only two or three steps of turning without losing the bend or flexion. This is a great way to re-establish balance as well as test the "in front of the leg" connection.

There are other lines where this can be tested. Riders can ride from the wall half a ten-meter circle, collecting the canter as they approach centerline, and then turn a couple steps of pirouette and ride back out of it back to the wall. There is the figure mentioned earlier from the Fourth Level Test 2 where the turning steps represent the tip of the V between the two diagonal lines. Turns across the arena, say from E to B, is another line.

Additionally, a walk pirouette can include a transition into tiny trot steps, and then a transition into canter pirouette and after a few steps of canter pirouette, the rider can then choose to ride out of it or, if it feels good, go for a few more steps. It's important all along to have that ability to ride out of it when the rider decides.

When the horse becomes more confident and strong, the number of turning steps can be increased until the horse can perform a full pirouette. When this is possible, the rider can fine tune the controls. For example, can the rider decide how long a step the horse takes with the inside hind within the exercise? Say, make it bigger, and then make it smaller? To ride the full pirouette "on a dinner plate" exactly on the center line is an impressive feat to be admired and applauded. It truly represents incredible technical skill of the rider, and strength and balance from the horse.

While losing the "in front of the leg" connection is a common mistake, it is not the only mistake. Horses that lose balance, fall behind the leg or simply tire, often try to use the neck (which is after all their "balancing arm") to help themselves lift the forehand and make the turn. So, if a horse moves the neck up and down excessively or comes above the bit they are perhaps trying hard, but not "there" yet.

When horses begin to struggle, it is common for riders to tip forward in the hip joint. It's hard to avoid this if the horse suddenly fell behind the leg or ran out of gas, but tipping forward and tightening the leg or hip can actually block the horse rather than help. The same can be true of rider's contact that is unsteady or backward.

As always, the collection has to begin with a driving aid, become contained by the seat and the moderating rein aid, and never begun with the reins. The state of the neck always gives information as to the state of the back. A tight neck tightens the back and impedes the ability for the hind leg to step under and take the weight. A good soft neck allows the back to lift, the hind leg to step under, and the ribcage to expand. The horse actually seems to get fatter between the legs of the rider, as if they have inflated. While a canter pirouette may not have the splashy look of an extended trot or the proud look of passage or the playful skipping look of one-tempis, they should be appreciated for the masterful display that they are.

Part Four: Commitment to Excellence

Catching the Corners

Riders tend to think of the progression of dressage exercises as only including exercises explicitly asked for in the tests. And that is, of course, not entirely wrong. But, the truth is that there are four exercises in every lap of the arena that are not explicitly asked for in the test; they are the four corners of the arena. How the corners are navigated speaks volumes about both horse and rider.

Corners well negotiated rebalance the horse, re-engage the hindquarter, and give the rider time to re-establish qualities that may have been lost from mishaps as well as give time to prepare the horse for what comes next. When tests are going badly, clever riders can "make the corners last" in order to regroup. When the corner lessons have not been well established and things go wrong (as they invariably will from time to time) the corners tend to whiz by as lost opportunities. A good test will feel like there is all the time in the world to prepare for the next exercise. Poor tests feel that the moment for preparation happened three strides behind you.

"Catch every corner" is a good motto to remember in every ride. Like everything else in dressage, "catching the corner" has to be trained from the beginning and become habit. It takes awareness followed by relentless discipline. Horses who are taught to "address" every corner in every ride will eventually anticipate the half-halt that happens prior to entering each corner and begin to rebalance themselves by habit.

When watching Reiner Klimke ride in the Los Angeles Olympics, I noted how Ahlerich came back from an extended canter at the end of the long side with Klimke yielding the reins. At the time, it seemed like magic. Nowadays, I understand that Ahlerich had been trained to collect prior to the corner. Because of this training, Klimke could close his legs to drive the horse's hind legs deeper under the body and actually soften his reins, which of course kept the neck and back of the horse unconstrained and rounded.

The corners should be thought of like a quarter of a circle. How small a circle depends on the level of the horse. There is no value of forcing a horse to go deeper into the corner than he can keep his balance. Horses that lose balance in the corners will always stiffen and lean and sometimes even trip. But, by Training Level Test 1, a horse has to be able to negotiate a turn down the center line, which is half of a ten-meter circle. This means that corners, which are merely a quarter of a ten meter circle, should be manageable at trot by the time a horse enters Training level. However, horses in Training level are only asked to canter on twenty-meter turns because at canter, even a quarter of a ten-meter circle is usually too difficult.

While a Training level horse will only be asked to canter on a twenty-meter bending line, and trot a ten-meter corner, as training progresses, the expectation is that the corners will be ridden in a balance that reflects that advancement. A Grand Prix horse would be expected to stay perfectly upright and bending on a corner that demonstrates the bend of a six-meter circle. Since a Grand Prix horse can canter or piaffe a pirouette, a six-meter bend is appropriate and should not be difficult.

Riders can begin to train the corners with transitions between and within the gaits, in the same way that the half-halt was first taught. Prior to "entering" the corner, the rider can walk or even halt for a step and then briskly ride back forward. This is repeated until the transition is not completed, but "aborted" and instead becomes a trained rebalancing half-halt.

Riders can approach the corner in shoulder-fore, activating the inside hind to step more deeply under the center of mass. Horses that fall through the inside bending leg can be corrected by using the inside leg to outside rein to teach them to "stand up" and shift the weight to the outside shoulder instead of leaning on the inside shoulder.

Riders can practice exiting the corner with a step of medium so that the engagement gained from the bend is used to lift the forehand as the corner is exited (this is excellent preparation for the first medium trot that happens on the diagonal in many tests).

Riders can train the corners with the help and guidance of traffic cones placed as "gates" which create visual guides for both horse and rider. Gates are strict! Depending on how tight they are placed they close any evasive "wiggle-room" where the horse deviated from the line of travel.

How the corner is trained must reflect where the horse happens to be in the training at the moment, as well as any problems the rider wants to address. Riders need to feel what is appropriate. But the goal is the same. The rider wants the end result to be that the horse, as it approaches the corner, is straight relative to the line of travel. The horse must then perform a rebalancing half-halt, bend and follow the curved line of that quarter of a circle and then must exit the corner straight and uphill with impulsion.

It's important to remember that "repetition is the mother of all learning." And that it is up to the rider to have focus before that same amount of focus can be expected of the horse.

Remember the Center Line (And All Those Other Lines)

It's important as dressage riders to look at the dressage arena, not as only a rectangle, but a rectangle dissected by many lines. The center line bisects the arena in half, the long way. The E/X/B line bisects the arena across the middle. But there are also the quarter lines that run the length of the arena between the center line and the wall.

Diagonal lines can be ridden at different angles from a corner of the long sides; the rider can choose to ride the full diagonal, three-quarter, or the half diagonal. Short diagonals can be ridden from lines like from "R" to "V". Diagonal lines can be ridden from the center line or quarter lines, too, toward the wall or back toward center line or over to the next quarter line.

Turns "across the middle" can be made between all the letters of the long sides of the arena, bisecting the center line at K/D/F, at V/L/P, E/X/B, S/I/R and H/G/M. All these lines merely sum up the possible straight lines available to the rider when training in the full arena. When you add circles and half circles of differing sizes, the options become nearly endless.

The rider has to be able to "see" these invisible lines by looking up and through the ears of the horse, drawing those imaginary lines in the sand and putting that line right between the front toes of the horse (or as in shoulder-in, the hind toes). As mentioned previously, riders need to "aim before they shoot."

From Training Level Test 1 to the Grand Prix, riders begin and end each test by riding center line to the halt and salute. In the beginning, it's easy to overlook training center line; that is until you try and practice the test! At that point, it can be a rude awakening at the level of difficulty involved.

A well ridden center line gives the judge the opportunity to award a high score. (Believe it or not, most judges want to be able to use the scale and give high marks.) Center lines are not, generally speaking, considered a brilliant or technically difficult movement, but the score still counts just as much as any of the other judged boxes (without co-efficients). This means that rider's have to buckle-down and do the "time on the center line" which isn't exactly exciting, but pays off later.

Riding center lines requires a horse to be straight without the support of the wall or fence. Like all the work, the more advanced the training, the easier it is to ride a straight center line, since hind legs that are well placed under the rider lighten the shoulders and make the horse easier to maneuver. Hind legs that are "unloaded" can "fishtail" rather than follow the line of travel by staying under the center of mass. Horses that are heavy on the forehand also can fall inside the line of travel by leaning onto the inside rein and shoulder in the turn. The better the balance and activity, the better the turn and the straighter the horse can be on center line.

Halts at "X" (or later at "I" or "G") should land straight and in good balance with the rider's leg in line with the "E/X/B" line that cuts across the middle of the arena. In other words, X marks the spot where the stirrup falls, not the nose or the tail of the horse. The horse should stand immobile for three full seconds (USEF rule!) for the salute (rider takes reins in the left hand, drops right hand and head in a quick salute, and then takes back up the reins). The move off should be crisp and without walk steps (at least, after Training level). The turn at C should be well prepared and, like the corners, appropriate in degree of bend to the level.

It can be helpful at home to train with the traffic cones set up on center line as gates, both for marking X, and for planning where to begin the turn at C. Having a mirror on your short side is especially helpful, not just for seeing deviations in straightness, but also for training the rider's eyes and bodyweight. The seat and bodyweight of the rider is influenced in subtle but influential ways by "looking up and between the ears." By learning to look up center line and at the judge (whether they are there or not) the rider centers themselves and helps balance the horse laterally.

Of course, the horse show environment always "ups the ante" since horses now have to negotiate the center-line work with judges and scribes, blowing tents and all sorts of other challenges. But still, it helps to have a plan, work the plan, and be willing to adapt or even ditch the plan to suit the horse you have on the day, versus the horse you have at home; but more on that later.

Working on center line always tests whether the horse is honestly "between the legs and reins" and of course, "in front of the leg." Horses not "in front of the leg" learn very quickly to anticipate the halt at "X" and can nearly give the rider whiplash or chip their teeth by making the downward transition before their rider. Horses that don't keep their internal engine on "high idle" in the (immobile) halt and continue to "think forward" can grow roots, lift up off the contact to see the big scary world, and then decide they have stage fright and want to go home. "Time on the center line," helps prevent this by practicing keeping the horse "on duty" throughout the exercise.

The center line is also a great place to practice shoulder-in and haunches-in. Once riders can control the line of travel, then it is fun to try switching from one direction to the other, or switching from one exercise to the other, checking how well the rider can accurately "hold the line."

Again, a mirror on the short side is a wonderful tool to have to confirm accuracy, but gates set up between are very strict taskmasters, too, that give immediate feedback. For example, if you set up one gate for the turn onto center line, another at X, and a final gate before the turn off center line, the cones will demand an accurate turn, then you can make a shoulder-in (for example) straighten to ride forward through the gate at X, and then make a shoulder-in the other direction, straighten before the last gate, and ride an accurate turn off of center line. The options are nearly endless.

Riding quarter lines are useful for beginning the zigzags. If riders have mirrors on the short side, quarter lines are also great lines to train the flying changes, especially when riders are training the tempi changes. Riders can clearly see any crookedness in the change as they ride straight on toward the mirror and work to "hold the line." As changes get straighter, they always get better. As horses get more advanced in the flying changes, riding the different lines not only tests the straightness, it helps keep the horse keen and listening instead of anticipating the changes every time they turn onto the long diagonal.

Changes performed on twenty-meter circles are also a great way to test balance. Trying to hold an accurate twenty-meter circle while performing tempi changes is a great test of balance and engagement, and a test for the rider of how well they can coordinate their aids; it's one of those "rub your belly while patting your head" kind of tests!

When riders use the different lines of the arena in a creative way, they can discover lines that ride especially well and bring out the best in the horse. These should be remembered for the day when horse and rider are ready to tackle a musical freestyle and can then be worked into the choreography.

Evaluating Progress

It is counter-productive to place too much importance on the ride you had today. Everyone has a day where they feel they did not do justice to the horse or that the horse did not feel as good as they had previously. The horse is not a machine and the only way they have to communicate with us is by demeanor and behavior; horses as much as people have some days that are better than others. Riders should honor that. But, on the other hand, riders need to know, not just feel, that they are progressing. Progress comes over time, but how much time? And what questions should riders ask themselves to evaluate progress?

Here are three good questions to ask:

1. Is my horse looking more beautiful?

A dressage horse in a good program gains top line. With correct training, the neck takes on an arched and wedge shape, with the widest part of the "wedge" at the base of the neck and the narrowest point right behind the ears. The bottom muscles (the muscles of resistance) of the neck get smaller and softer with good training and the top muscles (part of the long back muscles) get bigger. Horses who break in the wrong part of the neck show the widest part or a bulge a third of the way down the neck (from the ears).

There is also a part of the horse's back dressage riders call "the bridge." It begins at the last rib and stops at the pelvis. While this is often dropped or hollow in a young horse, it later fills in. The same can be said of the muscles along the spine that are now lifting and carrying the rider instead of sagging. Horses in good programs will score well on the standard "body condition" scale. They will have good energy and will glow with good health. Their feet will show good quality, too.

2. Are my horse's gaits improving?

A horse in a good program always progressively moves better as they progress and the gaits should never deteriorate. The walk should remain four-beat, and the canter three-beat. The trot should change the most as the power of the hind leg with improved balance over a proper connection to the bit adds swing and bounce to the stride. The canter should become straighter and find ease and stamina as it finds balance.

3. Is submission improving?

A horse should become calmer and more obedient as it understands and feels able to do the job it is asked to do. The more advanced the horse, the more it is under the control of the rider. There will certainly always be moment where a horse can get frightened or confused but, as the training progresses this, too, should get better and small lapses should become shorter and more quickly resolved.

These changes happen over time because of the quality of the entire program. Meaning: The horse should be handled competently in the stable as well as under saddle. The horse must be provided good nutrition and farrier and vet care as well as being ridden and trained well.

It helps for riders to ask themselves these questions and to look and think about the progress at about twelve-week intervals in order to give your program time to work. Keeping a journal helps the rider to be honest, too, since if you went away on vacation and your horse was a couch potato for ten days, it is simply not fair to blame the "program" when there was no "program" for those days.

I have created my own journal with short articles and beautiful photographs, but a plain lined notebook or calendar works, too.

Going Deeper into the Exercises

To have a horse understand the exercises to the point of performing with a measure of ease is a huge accomplishment. But the job is not done at that point, and no laurels can be "sat upon." Most of the exercises are shaped gradually over time, with the trainer rewarding "approximations," (The exception being teaching the flying change). Because of this process of shaping, no exercise is really a finished product until you are confirmed at Grand Prix. So, for example, a rider may be able to fulfill the line of half-pass that is required in Third level Test 3 and be able to score a "7" which is the score for "fairly good." But, while that's cause for satisfaction, the half-pass will have a different look and feel by the time the horse has moved up to the FEI levels. It helps to watch the "best of the best" perform the trot and canter half-passes (and other exercises) at Grand Prix to be both impressed and to "set the minds eye" to the highest standards. We can all dream. And since humans learn multiple ways, "seeing" is an important tool to incorporate into the educational mix, and fun besides. Imitation and modeling are subtle ways for riders to use the power of the mind to shape themselves.

In order to take the exercises "to the next level" requires that a rider continue to improve the balance and suppleness, the reactions, the submission, and the control in and out of and within the exercises. But especially it is the development of strength that makes the biggest difference. The quality of the gaits will be reflected in the quality of the exercises. Remember, if the gaits deteriorate, then the program needs re-evaluating.

Of course, strength building doesn't come overnight. If you compare strength training for the horses to human weight training at the gym, it becomes clear how incrementally you increase the intensity, but at the same time, how relentless you have to be about staying consistent.

At the gym, when one weight feels easy, its time to add more. At the same time, if you add too much too soon, at worst, you risk injury and minimally you make yourself sore. And while humans can mentally justify muscle soreness, horses cannot. They just know they hurt. It also becomes clear that not every day can be at the same intensity or drill the same exercise. Muscles need warm up and recovery and days of rest. Most dressage injuries come from over drilling and from pushing on in a moment of fatigue. It's good to keep that in mind as you make a plan and work the plan.

Things take time. This isn't a reason to be discouraged, it's a reason to stay inspired and mentally engaged in the process. Even horses who are not gifted with a lot of scope will surprise the rider and sometimes even themselves when they feel strong in their bodies and full of life. Riders can have a "where did that come from?" moment when the horse expresses joi de vive with an extra bouncy step or lift in the shoulders. But, those special moments don't come by themselves; they come from a rider playing the "thinking" game as they explore variations and approaches within and between the exercises. Those moments can only come from a horse who is fit and healthy and mentally engaged.

Playing the "thinking game" requires creativity. It keeps the sessions interesting for both horse and rider. I think it highly unfair to expect horses to "focus" one hundred percent on the rider when the rider is not paying attention to them. While it's just fine to take a hack on loose reins and enjoy nature and chat with your best buddy about weekend plans, it's totally unfair to have that chat with your buddy while "working" the horse and especially if the rider should get mad at the horse if it should "look out the classroom window" or lose focus in any other way when it was the rider who lost focus first. When a rider "takes up the reins" they should expect the horse to focus and "go to the office" to work. But, the rider owes the horse the same mental discipline. It doesn't mean work should be drudgery, but it does take focus.

Approaches to "going deeper into the exercise" are nearly endless. Here is an example to improve the lift and carry in medium canter along with improving the level of collection in and out of the medium canter: Ride a very collected counter-canter through the short sides, and then out of the corners, being careful to keep the shoulders right up against the wall, ride medium canter in counter-canter down the long sides.

The level of collection required to navigate the counter-canter through the short sides, along with the straightness required to ride the counter-canter in medium canter along the wall, should produce a wonderful feel in the medium canter with increased balance and power. If the rider is successful, they can even try to turn from the short side in counter-canter, across the diagonal into a medium or extended canter (be sure to leave room to collect before the next corner which will now be in true canter). While this is an example of a fairly advanced exercise, this "thinking game" to improve the medium canter applies just as easily to an exercise from the lower levels.

Here is an example to improve the leg yield: The rider can ride leg yield from the beginning of the long wall to quarter line, ride trot lengthening for a few steps and then ride leg yield back to the wall.

When the rider changes the direction of leg yield, the exercise helps keep the horse "centered" between both legs and reins, preventing the "falling through" of the stabilizing effect of the outside rein or leg. This "falling through" creates unbalance, rather than increasing balance.

Here is another variation, the rider can begin across the diagonal in leg yield, following the diagonal line precisely with the shoulders of the horse, then straighten the horse on the diagonal and ride four steps in trot lengthening, and after four steps ride back again to leg yield, once again the rider can straighten the horse on the diagonal out of the leg yield and finish the line in trot lengthening. The rider should use their eyes on the focal point of the letter at the end of the diagonal line to be dead-on accurate and prove they have control of the shoulders with the outside rein. At the same time, this exercise tests the response to the rider's sideways-driving leg aid as well as testing that the horse remains "in front of the leg." Riders should feel easily how riding the exercise improves the quality of the trot. This is the touchstone to every exercise.

These are two examples of reaching into a "tool box wide and deep" that all riders need to develop for themselves through the "thinking game." If you understand mechanics and you have "installed the controls," then there is never a reason to become too frustrated or confused and certainly no reason to ever be bored. Remember the adage, "Ask often, expect little, reward generously."

But I also like the saying, "You no-asky, you no-getty." And "the definition of insanity is doing the same thing over and over, expecting different results." I once had a new student say to me that she thought dressage was about "going round and round a twenty-meter circle, where nothing ever changes." She was soon apprised of a different reality!

Riders usually can bring more quality to every exercise by using their minds and their creativity instead of riding harder or stronger. There is the old saying that "when all you have is a hammer, every problem looks like a nail." Without engaging the mind, riders will get frustrated and instead override, using stronger aids or equipment, when really all they needed was to reach into the toolbox and use a different tool.

It is amazing sometimes how a new approach will get a response from the horse where they seem to say, "Well, if that's all you wanted, why didn't you say so in the first place?"

Taking It On The Road

There is something exhilarating about loading up your horse and heading out on a road trip. It's a tremendous amount of work. The weather rarely seems to cooperate, regardless of the season. No matter how well prepared, there will be unforeseen mishaps. And when the trip is over, there will be complete and utter exhaustion and something else, too. Is it the euphoria of having simply survived? Something of value does happen, regardless of the scores received or the color of the ribbons. Perhaps it's a variation of the "foxhole syndrome," but it is real nonetheless: you and your horse have come closer to each other in a way that doesn't happen in the comfort of home. You will both be tested and, by coming through the "test," learn to depend on each other.

While the rider must always be the one calling the shots and shouldering the burden of leadership, horses are usually different away from home. That's not always negative. A phlegmatic horse can sometimes light up in a good way in a strange place. An insecure horse can sometimes draw inward and feel relieved to "let Jesus take the wheel." A horse that is bossy at home can suddenly need the rider to tell them what to do and be sweetly calling the rider back to the stall should they wander too far away.

A little stress reveals a lot about character (every person in a marriage knows this!). A little stress when handled well makes any relationship stronger. And since nothing builds success like success, it's important to plan roads trips so that the challenges that can be planned will be surmountable and can develop both a resilient horse and a resilient rider. Of course, not all challenges can be planned. That's part of the "wild ride" that I write about in my novels. The best "inoculation" to protect your health and sanity for those unforeseen rides is to train, train, train, train. Even then, there will always be something unplanned to test horse and rider and it rarely has to do with riding the dressage test.

Clinics are a fun and collegial way to begin taking trips away from home. It gives horses a chance to work in a strange environment without the stress of having a judge award a public score for the performance. There is usually much to be learned from watching and listening to everyone else's session as well as yours, and riders who only ship in for their session and then leave miss out.

Many trainers bring in outside trainers for private clinics at their home farm. These are sometimes hard to find and often are filled with that trainer's own students, but outside riders can sometimes get in if a spot opens. GMOs (Group Member Organizations of USDF) often bring in clinicians that are available for "first come/first served" for members, and your check reserves your spot.

USDF runs separate clinics for adult riders and for young riders in most regions. Being a USDF member provides opportunities to ride in these clinics or to volunteer to be a demonstration rider for one of their educational programs. Being a demo rider means being willing to demonstrate whatever is asked and to take comments in good spirit even if you think they are harsh. To avoid those sorts of negative experiences, it helps to demonstrate a level that you and your horse are performing with ease.

Programs cannot be run without riders willing to submit themselves to the process, and the horses don't know and don't care about the critiques and so always can benefit from the outing.

It also helps to know before you sign up, just what/who you are signing up for/with. With the internet, it's easy to watch someone teach and to hear a bit about the personality and character of the clinician. There are plenty of good and knowledgeable people out there teaching who are genuine and respectful and want to make you and your horse better. There is no reason to sign up to ride with someone who has a reputation for being abrasive or (God forbid) abusive. To be a good teacher, you must enjoy working with people as well as horses. I have been stunned to find that some out there taking nice-size checks do not seem to enjoy one or the other or sometimes both.

And while I am always interested and open to seeing trainers who are lauded as excellent in other disciplines (I love to watch work at liberty, and I love vaulting, and yes, I love cavaletti work, and more). It can be a real mistake to sign up for a clinic with someone working in a totally non-standard system of training with its own set of bells and whistles, equipment, and often a DVD they will try to sell you while you are there. While there are many roads to Rome, if you want to go to Rome, it helps to point yourself in the direction of Rome. In other words, work with someone who is already successful at what you want to become successful doing. It sounds obvious, but there is always someone re-inventing a new version of dressage and it's wise to use caution to avoid wasting time and money, or worse.

Organizing and running clinics is a lot of work but, as in anything in life, if you don't see what you need being offered in your area, the answer is to step in and do it yourself.

USDF Adult Camps are another horse "adventure" that I wish were more available. I taught at one (and I brought my own horse) and I had as much fun as any of the campers. I realize USDF Adult Camps take a lot of planning and it's not easy to find an appropriate venue or to keep costs reasonable, but I highly recommend the experience and encourage anyone who wants to organize one in their area to have a go at it. (USDF offers a workbook to organizers.)

Even when horse and rider are feeling good about the work at home and have ventured forth into the world to road test the horse and rider, it's still not simple to enter a show and produce a successful ride. Test riding and producing your best test at the show is a separate skill from simply advancing the training. I am in awe of those riders who seem to have mastered test riding. I am in awe as well of those riders who ride just as well (or better) at a show as they do at home. I envy those supremely confident people who are 100% there for their horses and never tighten up or override because they are being judged. We all wish we could have the confidence of a Deb; but most of us are more like Lizzy, full of self-doubt and anxiety which means we have to create "self-talk" and other preparation that allows us to perform at our best, even under scrutiny.

Some of the top riders out there surprisingly are as anxiety filled as the rest of us; they are not super-human, but they have learned how to manage their stress. The best defense is to be prepared and to be sure to enter a test that does not over challenge either horse or rider. In other words, if the test is not easy at home, enter an easier test. There is no better way to develop confidence than to experience success, no matter how small.

Finding comfort in situations that are by design uncomfortable is one of the challenges of showing. To me, this means things like only showing in well broken-in boots and a helmet that is so comfortable that I forget it is on. My hair-do and gloves and stock-tie all better be comfy, too. The same is true for my horse in that I do not want stiff show pads, never-washed polo wraps, or stiff new leather girths or reins. I also want my horse to rest, and I know that horses have to learn how to rest at the shows instead of feeding off the stressors and becoming exhausted by staying continually on high-alert. While I can't eliminate the stressors that are a natural part of the environment of a showground, I can provide a nice deep bed of shavings that at least encourages them to lie down.

Discovering the best routine for your horse takes practice and "getting it wrong" a few times in order to figure it out. Once you think you have it figured out, it can change as the horse relaxes in the show environment and needs less warm up time. Each horse is an individual and may need more or less hand-walking, or lungeing or riding time. All this takes time to discover and is part of the game.

To get the best results at a show at any level, it helps to take the test apart at home and well in advance of entering. It's good to be sure that each part is "do-able" separately before worrying about making each exercise flow smoothly to the next one. When the rider and horse do run through the test from "salute to salute" it's important that they do so in a nonjudgmental and casual manner where "do-overs" are allowed. First ride throughs are not for demonstrating power or perfection but for figuring out strategies on how best to get from point to point. I often have riders add ten-meter circles in every corner when first riding a "run-through" so they give themselves "thinking time." Sometimes in test riding, trainer and rider discover trouble spots in the test and then can come up with a clever approach that solves the problem.

An example is the First level change of canter lead on the diagonal over "X" through a few steps of trot. Changing leads on a straight line can be a balance challenge for a green horse. So, instead, say on the left lead, the rider begins to canter across the diagonal and, before reaching X, rides a ten-meter circle to the left and makes a transition to trot prior to reaching X. At X the rider makes a ten-meter circle to the right picking up the right lead canter and then finishes the diagonal in right lead canter.

Horses soon learn to anticipate the circle and organize themselves onto the hindquarters, making a self-imposed rebalancing "half-halt." When this becomes habit, the rider will find they can now smoothly execute the change of lead through the trot leaving out the circles as they canter across the diagonal. But, if riders do not begin the preparation for the test well in advance, of course, there is no time to "train" the correct response and instead riders are more inclined to get frustrated (and pull on reins, etc.)

Schooling shows are another way to test rider and horse to be sure both are adequately prepared to enter a recognized show. Recognized shows are expensive and scores earned become part of the permanent record for both horse and rider. That makes a schooling show result unimportant except for the experience and the valuable feedback. Judges for schooling shows are usually "L" graduates and so the scores should be an honest reflection of where your performance would score at a recognized show. Schooling show judges who over-reward do a huge disservice to those who are there as preparation for recognized shows. I think it is important to know the venue of the schooling show ahead of entering so that footing and stabling (if stabling is offered) is a known quantity.

Videotaping your test at home is also a great tool. I think it is good to videotape lessons and regular training rides, too, if you have the ability to do so. While some things are less exciting to see on a videotape (the video can't capture the thrill of riding an extended trot) it can provide excellent information that can make huge impacts on riders. It also can be tremendously reassuring. The inner dialogue that riders have often has little basis in reality. Watching yourself on video can tamp down negativity and reset the voice of your inner critic to one who notices the good bits as much as the bad bits. I love the new video cameras that don't need an operator, but follow a button the rider wears: definitely on my wish list.

When you have found your "test" and are satisfied with your "run through" then it's time to find a show to enter. It's important to belong to both USDF and USEF if you are planning to "get into the game" of recognized shows. You will need to have your horse also "registered" or at least sign up for a temporary horse ID number. Horses can be

"Lifetime Registered" with both organizations. Either way, the horse is assigned a number for life. All scores earned are then tracked with that horse and provide a proof of show record. These association fees can add up, so it's important to join up well ahead of actually entering in order to avoid "sticker shock" of paying for all of it at one time.

All horses must have a negative EIA (Coggins) test provided with the entries and that also must be carried with the horse at all times. Coggins tests need to be updated every year. Horses must have up to date vaccination records with them and available on request. FEI horses that are entering CDI classes must have a well-maintained FEI passport to present to the ground jury on the day of the soundness jog. When crossing state lines, most states also require a health certificate. These health certificates are good for 30 days, six months, or in some states one year. If you are crossing state lines, be sure to check on the required paperwork well in advance of the trip and whether you are required to stop at the state line like you must do to enter Florida. It's not fun to see blue lights in your rearview mirror while you are hauling horses.

I believe all recognized horse shows now may be entered on line. If you are planning to try and qualify for any Championships, then be sure to read the fine print about the requirements. The USDF Regional Championships are accessible for most everyone who can meet the minimum scores and, while there is an extra fee (and the score has to come from Test 3) once you are qualified, you no longer have to pay the fee. It's a nice "feather in your cap" to be able to have qualified at the level regardless of whether you decide to compete at "Regionals." Of course, you don't need to pay the qualifying fee if you know for certain you don't want to go to Regionals.

Grooms are nice to take along (also known as friends or family members who actually know how to handle a horse). But, not everyone has the luxury of a groom. If you have a group from your barn or trainer's barn to join, it makes it a social event and the extra support is always welcome. It's also nice to pay the extra fee for a tack room (if available). The expense can often be divided through sharing.

Getting the hang of showing takes practice, a great deal of energy, planning, preparation and, of course, funds. With a few shows under your belt you begin to figure out what you need to do your best. Do you put in your own braids or pay for a professional job? Do you hate motel pillows and need to bring your own? Coffee-maker, yes or no? Food from home or food from the concession stand? You find through trial and error the best and lightest way to tote the gazillion things you must "schlep" to set up your stall and tack room. And don't forget the hose and nozzle and a safe way to tie your horse. I, of course, keep "Emma's" laminated list with a dry erase marker to check off each item as I pack. Be sure to check the hitch, the lights, the brakes, and the hitch—again. Keep the trailer serviced and the tires inflated and checked for dry rot. Same advice goes for the truck.

And try not to make yourself ill with "road food" or too sleepy on long trips. Whatever the results, remember that you have a horse, you lucky person you.

The Man In The Arena—Excerpt from the speech "Citizenship in a Republic" delivered at the Sorbonne, in Paris, France on 23 April, 1910 By President Theodore Roosevelt

> *It is not the critic who counts;* not the man who points out how the strong man stumbles, or where the doer of deeds could have done them better. The credit belongs to the man who is actually in the arena, whose face is marred by dust and sweat and blood; who strives valiantly; who errs, who comes short again and again, because there is no effort without error and shortcoming; but who does actually strive to do the deeds; who knows great

enthusiasms, the great devotions; who spends himself in a worthy cause; who at the best knows in the end the triumph of high achievement, and who at the worst, if he fails, at least fails while daring greatly, so that his place shall never be with those cold and timid souls who neither know victory nor defeat.

I love this famous excerpt from a Teddy Roosevelt speech. I love it so much, it hangs in my tack room. I know that I will never be considered among the "cold and timid souls" because of what my riding has taught me and I believe that, as a group, riders cannot belong to such a group. We practice leadership every day in every ride. We also take those lessons from riding out into our non-riding life.

But, I also love the quote because in dressage we always fail to meet the high standards that have been set in the sport. Once you understand the standard and what "excellent" or a score of "10" requires, you become painfully aware of inadequacies. You now understand every intractable flaw that exists in your beloved partner, your horse. You see yourself on video or in a photo and read the comments made by the judge regarding why you and your horse are not deserving a higher score, perhaps after you just performed your personal best. Despite this, each of us has to find a way to persevere and do it in a way that recognizes the value of our horse and ourselves. We cannot let the "critic" erode our joy, the love of our animal, or our own sense of worth.

The ability to persevere and maintain "great enthusiasm" and "great devotion" regardless of the sweat and toil and yes, even some blood on occasion, is what defines the kind of person we become. Not bitter, not proud, but able to find reward in our dedication, discipline, and honest effort.

I promise that if riders stay in the game long enough, they will suffer great disappointments. Everyone will eventually have something go so wrong that the score will come back low enough to scorch your innards. Yes. That bad.

Whenever someone I know suffers through one of those rides, I tell them my story. I once had a ride so terrible that I should have asked to be excused but was too inexperienced to know to do it and soldiered on when I shouldn't have (the horse got his tongue over the bit, curled the neck down and was barely steerable). After a red-faced salute, the judge told me that I was "an embarrassment to the sport of dressage" and awarded me a score of 46%. I still have the urge to defend myself when I bare my soul and repeat his comment and that score, but I won't. It was just awful on so many levels, but it happened.

After all these years, I can't forget that comment or that score, but what I soon learned is that no one else remembers it. (Of course, now you all know!) The truth is that the other competitors are wrapped up in their own performances and don't care about my public humiliation. The breeders and owners are wrapped up in their own horses. The trainers are caught up in getting all their clients to the arenas and functioning. The judges are checking their watches to stay on schedule and hoping something good comes into their arenas to wake them back up. (Judging is a long day where, depending on the season, you freeze, roast, eat dust, or drown.) My own personal misery didn't kill me. And it didn't stop me. And when your turn comes, don't let it stop you either.

Along with the embarrassment of receiving a low score is the inward embarrassment of the too-high score. While a "gift" score doesn't kick you in the gut like a low score, it does make you cringe. Once you are well trained on the standard and know what a "6" versus a "7" or "8" rides or looks like, you also know when your score was simply too high. At a certain point, you can guess fairly closely after your final salute where you should score. And while it's bad form to denigrate a "gift," it can get uncomfortable as your friends rush to congratulate you. High scores often make judges popular, but for those riders who don't realize they have just been over rewarded, the ultimate awarding of an accurate score can feel harsh.

Discipline: The Secret Sauce

Everything I've ever accomplished turned out to be harder than I thought it would be, took longer than I thought it should, and cost more than I thought I could afford. But, self-delusion has its benefits. Beginnings are "blind" and it's a good thing they are. (How would anyone ever become a parent otherwise?) Fate gives us this incredible ability to be in utter self-denial of the odds of achieving our goals or understanding the difficulty of what we have set in front of ourselves as we step off into our great adventures.

When I decided to write a novel, I was fortunate to jump out of the gate with just such naive enthusiasm. But, just like training a horse, at some point I had to slow down and actually study. (And I already had a degree in Creative Writing). Then came the "donkey work" of "taking the time it takes" to secure a foundation and to build from there. The "donkey work" was not exciting. In fact, I had to set the timer on my oven clock and force myself to work without looking up from the screen until the timer went off.

When you start a new horse, all things seem possible. "This" horse is better than any you had before. "This" horse is going to climb up the levels and be a child progeny. And it's important to believe it, too. A famous rider was asked at a clinic, "Which of your horses is your favorite?" His answer was, "Whatever horse I am sitting on." What a beautiful answer! He invested himself into each horse he rode with belief, and in the long run, what matters if his belief was justified in fact or slightly delusional? With an attitude like that, riders are well armed to carry on when that initial dream and its attendant enthusiasm runs smack into reality.

Not every day, month, or year, is going to feel successful. There may be a day that you find yourself sitting on the ground watching "this" beautiful horse bucking down the long side without you. There has to be a reason to keep going. Some people seem to be born with incredible self-discipline preinstalled. There are people who ooze self confidence and never seem plagued by doubt. There is an inner drive that pushes them onwards until a sense of completion or just complete exhaustion is attained.

I'm not going to claim to be such a person by nature. I hate falling off. I hate to be embarrassed in public. I'm not a genius in the saddle, and I am no "horse whisperer." In my lowest moments, I grumble that my horse "ought" to appreciate how well it is cared for and how much money I am spending on its comfort. (How stupid is that?) My horse still pins her ears at me when I go into her stall. How's that for appreciation? So much for that part of the fairytale.

Discipline to carry on is the glue that keeps things together and takes me on to the next level. It's what makes me pass on the peanut butter and chocolate-covered doughnut calling to me like a siren song from behind the counter where I just ordered my coffee.

I am no Marine Corps drill sergeant when it comes to discipline. I love to stay up late reading and sleep in. I hate running or going to the gym. I will eat potato chips and chocolate bars for dinner if left to myself too long. My saving grace is that I am stubborn; really, really, stubborn. And if I decide on a goal, then "Katie bar the door." With this streak of stubborn comes the ability to enforce habits that are not innate. It turns out that I can get up in the morning (if I need to), eat well (I sure miss potato chips and chocolate croissants) and even go to the gym (I still hate running).

The truth is that horse shows and awards are not enough to sustain anyone over the long course that training requires. I love being able to show off my horse, to spend time with other riders I enjoy, and to be rewarded with a good score. There are the great moments of victory, neck sashes, and award ceremonies, but those moments are fleeting. They are not enough to bring a rider through rough patches. And there will be rough patches. In those stretches, discipline to stick to the tried and true plan carries horse and rider forward. When faith is shaken, rely on discipline.

Horses do not hear the ticking of the clock the way that we do. They do not know what level you had planned to show or the sacrifices you have made in order to ride. But, by listening to the horses and devoting yourself to the daily disciplines, things proceed. Impatience or frustration may seem like they push things along faster, but generally they slow things down, because mistakes have to be repaired later. Flying changes are a perfect example. Riders who push ahead when the horse is simply not ready can confirm a change that is "late behind" and then need a year to undo the learned technique and reteach a correct change.

When riders become frustrated (and I guarantee that every rider will) it means that they have come to the end of their knowledge or skill level. This is not a bad thing since both knowledge and skill can be acquired IF the rider is willing to "do the donkey work" to acquire them. And doing that "donkey work" requires a great deal of discipline.

Riders feeling frustrated need to step back, play the "thinking game" to noodle things out instead of blaming the horse for not meeting expectations. Riders must manage their own expectations to avoid frustration because the horse has none. If riders are frustrated, they need to keep it to themselves so they do not poison the entire session with their own disappointments. This is where riders, instead of giving up, dedicate themselves to becoming a better rider tomorrow than they are today. How? By using the power of discipline.

It might mean more lessons, or more studying, more time without stirrups, or any other number of ways to advance knowledge and skill or one's own emotional state. It might mean forcing yourself to crack open the books. You can set the timer on your oven if it helps you keep the seat of your pants to the seat of your chair to take the time it takes.

The "secret sauce" is disciple, applied daily—stubbornly.

Speed Bumps, Road Blocks, and Heartbreaks

It's not easy to write this section, but it's something that I feel too many dressage texts leave out. If you ride and train long enough, you are bound to have your heart broken. If you are serious about riding and training, you cannot help but invest of yourself in the animal you are training. If you "go on the road" you not only spend your hour a day together, you spend countless hours together. The health and well-being of that animal gets tied into your own. I cannot honestly believe people who say they don't feel this way about their horses. I remember overhearing someone who was selling their 19-year-old horse say that she didn't want him to "die in her barn." It seemed at the time the coldest thing I had ever heard uttered. Later, much later, I realized the cold tone was masking the fact that she indeed, was not made of the "right stuff" emotionally to see her horse safely eased to his end. "Being there" until the end takes a lot of courage and a willingness to bear some mighty pain. To be in charge of a horse's well-being is a burden, but part of the package. Not everyone is emotionally equipped, but if you sign on for "the wild ride" it's best to read the fine print at the bottom of the page. You will at some point feel gutted.

Horses' lives are short and hopefully ours are going to be long. While we understand this in concept, it doesn't make the end any easier. Horses are just as fragile as we are. Additionally, they cannot be put, strictly speaking, into "bed rest" to recover from serious injuries. Horses, in order to survive, must be able to lie down and get up and move around. Horses are susceptible to fatal bouts of colic. Cushing's disease wreaks havoc and complications like founder often are unmanageable.

Horses as prey animals can cause terrible damage to themselves in moments of panic. You can try your best to prevent the worst and avoid most of the known dangers that hang over all of us who ride and keep horses. But no one can be ready for everything and things can go downhill in the blink of an eye. I lost my Wasabi to aflatoxin poisoning, most likely ingested in her feedstuff, although testing never located the source. I was blindsided to suddenly lose a perfectly healthy animal who was only ten years old. And of course, I had spent six years of riding her nearly every day and advancing her training, enduring the tough rides and being exhilarated by the good rides. But, although the reason for her death was unusual, losing her was not. When I send condolences to others who have suffered the loss of their horse, and I say, "I understand," it is because I do indeed understand.

Each foaling season I revel in the posted photos on social media of lovely newborn foals. They are the product of carefully planned breedings, and their arrivals have been anticipated from long before they were a little blob on an ultrasound. But each year I also see the posts of the foals who didn't make it, leaving distressed dams, as well as the mares who have perished, leaving fragile orphans. Life is fraught with peril and nature is cruel. But "tis better to have loved and lost, than never to have loved at all." To all those breeders who carry on through the heartbreak to provide riders lovely young horses that make our hearts beat faster, I send my genuine shout-out of gratitude.

These sad events, of course, cannot be allowed to haunt you forever or they would suck the pleasure right out of any future riding. The horse you ride today deserves better. To be successful and to find fulfillment in the daily process, riders have to be able to put on "emotional blinders" when they put their foot in the stirrup to mount. Horses live in the moment. Maybe that's one reason they are so good for us. To be as present in the moment as they are is one of the restorative gifts of riding and training. Riders cannot ride their best without learning to do this. That is not to say that grief is to be ignored or that heartbreak is something you ever "get over." A long life, well-lived, is not one that you finish unscathed. The really brave just keep getting back up after each hard knock and try to keep giving the best of themselves to whoever is still left standing there beside them.

Textbooks and videos on riding and training sometimes present the process like a smooth road, where riders advance from level to level, checking off the boxes as they go along. Trust me, this is rare. While experienced trainers proceed a lot quicker through the levels than new trainers, even experienced trainers hit bumps in the road. Sometimes the speed bump is a behavior problem that simply needs a clearer correction. Sometimes the horse needs to go back and reconfirm the basics, or the trainer needs to take another approach to the problem. Sometimes everyone needs to take a few days off or go for a hack and take all the pressure off. Sometimes it's a physical problem. In that case, it's time to call in the team and start from the shoes and work your way up to rule things out. Be sure and include the fit of all equipment in that process. It's important to rule out the possibility of pain or discomfort as the source of the problem, but it's also critical that once the physical is ruled out, to face the issue and not waste time making excuses.

There is absolutely no shame in getting help and advice no matter who you are or how experienced you are. Sometimes a rider is too close to the problem to see the solution. When you bring a horse along from the beginning, you tend to ride the horse you "used to have" instead of the horse you have now. Another good experienced rider can often get on without any preconceptions and address the horse in a fresh way that changes everything. Bumps in the road can feel frustrating, and may eat up a year working through, making the year one of "remedial" work rather than advancing to the next level. But, it is what it is and riding out those bumps is the only way forward. Have faith and keep going.

Road blocks are those things that stop the training. It's tough when your horse sustains an injury that takes them "out of the game" for an extended period. It's not uncommon for dressage horses to sustain ligament injuries. Ligaments are very slow healers and, if not healed properly and then rehabbed completely, can keep coming back. The best advice is to first try your best to avoid injury. Most injuries happen from overuse and overtraining. Shoeing imbalances can be at fault. As can working in too deep a footing. Sometimes injuries happen when the horse "hits the wall" and is fatigued and we misread the feeling and cause the injury. Some conformation faults lend themselves to these sorts of injuries. But once you find yourself sidelined, it's all hindsight, and while educational, not very reassuring to hear the cause. It helps no one at this point to engage in guilty self-flagellation. Ligament injuries are not the only physical roadblock you can find in your way; the list of reasons for a lay-up are many. The time does pass and for the obsessive rider it often helps if another "ride" can be found to fill some of the down time. There is always the dreaded gym.

Some road blocks are tougher. A dressage horse that never gets the flying change clean and on the aids is not going up the levels. A small tour horse (Prix St. Georges / Intermediate 1) that cannot learn the one-tempi changes is going to always be a small-tour horse. If your goal is large-tour Grand Prix, you have a decision to make. A horse who has given you all he is capable of giving you, for whatever reason, can still be a valuable horse for someone else. In that case, it can be the most responsible thing to sell your horse to someone who will benefit from and cherish the animal. There is nothing amiss with a horse who takes multiple riders up the levels, teaching riders to "outgrow" its level. The Schoolmaster or "Professor" horse is a valuable animal who, generally speaking, earns itself a fan club and is guaranteed a good home for life. That horse doesn't have to be a Grand Prix horse.

Wasabi, owned and ridden by Karen McGoldrick, photo by Sherry Smith
I purchased Wasabi as a four-year-old and trained her for six years when she suddenly became ill and died. It felt like a punch to the gut. A year later however, I found Gia and began a new journey. The alternative was unthinkable.

A Word About Insurance

While I can certainly understand that people who own multiple horses find the cost of insuring a "herd" to be prohibitive, for most of us who own one or two horses, it can be a financial lifesaver. I would hate to have money be the deciding factor in a medical emergency. I have used my equine mortality and major medical policy only once in my life. It was small consolation to be insured but, regardless of heroic and sadly fruitless efforts to save Wasabi, I at least was able to ultimately purchase another young horse.

What's It's All About?

I've always believed that approached the right way, the pursuit of dressage trains not only the horse but the person. Whatever a person lacks in their own character soon will become apparent. A timid person will learn courage, an impatient person will be forced to take "the time it takes," an arrogant person soon will be humbled. There is no "faking it" and it is fairly common to spot a novice horseman by their quickness to overstate their own ability. But, once they are aboard, the truth is there for all to see. Even a horse who "tolerates" bad riding well will never look and go the same for a mediocre rider as they do a good rider. The "trainer effect" of putting up a novice rider after a good rider gets off, generally only lasts a few trips around the arena, before the weaker rider "reshapes" the horse to their own level. (It's still a good idea, since for those few precious laps, before it wears off, the novice gets a glimpse of how it *can* feel.)

Horses go as they are ridden. The horse becomes a reflection of the rider. Even accounting for differences in conformation and temperament, it is typical that horses ridden and trained by "X" all take on a similar "way of going." If you are Carl Hester, well, that's great. If you are a less talented amateur whose horses are always having problems, then clearly, it's not. But when that same amateur's horse begins to improve, it means that the rider has made some important changes. Those changes, even technical improvements, start between the ears of the rider. The horse rewards the rider when they improve. (Horses always are honest in their assessments.) Those honest rewards are more meaningful than any ribbon.

It is true that growth is usually uncomfortable. Most riders have to "fail their way to success." Failure feels terrible. Failure is painful. Egos can bruise easily. But the moments of success are even more powerful and addictive. While success is not always delivered at a horse show, even if no one else is around, the horse is always there, part of the process, delivering immediate feedback. Those positive moments make up for the far greater moments where we feel inadequate. That's what keeps us all "at it."

People who refuse to submit themselves humbly to the process, to accept their own limits, and take the failures and discomfort as "de rigueur," not only do not improve, they rarely last. All the fancy "rigs" and mounts, the lovely clothes and custom boots, cannot make up for the "donkey work" required to develop real skill and deep satisfaction. When you see riders constantly selling horses and buying new ones or constantly switching trainers, then it seems safe to assume that the "search" that they are on is misdirected.

Dressage training is a pursuit that satisfies on many levels: dressage is a sport—dressage is an intellectual pursuit—dressage is an art.

Dressage is, of course, an athletic pursuit that is also an organized sport. For those who say that "the horse does all the work" I say, hop on the lunge line and sit the trot for me then tell me again how the horse does all the work. It is true that the better a rider becomes and the more advanced the horse becomes, the less taxing it becomes. A well balanced horse with a strong top line lifts and carries the rider in a way that feels terrific and comfy. A horse that loses balance and runs on his forehand feels terrible to sit.

Riders who ride a lot of horses every day invariably suffer wear and tear on joints. The biggest problem is lower back pain from compression. It's a good rule for dressage riders to touch their toes and reach for the sky every day, since even with long stirrups, hips and knees are bent and hamstrings can become too tight. Dressage riders must have strong core muscles but don't need a lot of strength in arms or legs. Dressage riders typically do not get adequate cardio workouts. So, even though it is a sport, it's smart to add additional stretching, cardio, and core-strength training to a rider's routine. However, I totally understand that if trainers have to sit on many horses a day, it's hard to have any time or energy left in the day for the gym.

Dressage is an intellectual pursuit. The first known treatise on dressage was written by the Greek philosopher Xenophon. It's still in print. And while it is not required reading for the understanding of modern dressage sport, it is indicative of the deep and long tradition we are part of as horsemen and women. The modern sport horse, while continually being refined for the job we ask of it, is still the same creature that Xenophon described. As humans, we have the unique ability for each generation to build on what has gone before us through the legacy of the printed word.

There is no reason to "reinvent the wheel" in each generation of horsemen. We should read. But there is also no need to malign new knowledge; else you get stuck in the wrong century, putting the old masters on an absurdly unattainable pedestal. There are excellent new books to read and lots of new information about horses and how they really move and how they learn and think. An improvement in saddles and bitting based on diagnostics that the old masters could only dream of is one example. Because of that, it's good to keep reading, to keep listening, to keep watching, and to stay open and thinking about what you read, hear, and see.

The sharing of ideas for the betterment and improvement of all is why we have conferences and symposiums and clinics. I think that as riders delve deeper into dressage study they want to know as much as they can. In the beginning, it's about solidifying the basic skills. Then it's about understanding the theory and system. Once riders take up teaching others, it's clear that those essentials have to be able to be put clearly into words. Acquiring that essential "toolbox, wide and deep" requires study. And not one single person "has it all." I loved when Margot stated that "the arrogance of the present ignores the intelligence of the past." It's a common fault of youth in really any endeavor, but easy to spot in the sport of dressage.

Dressage, in its best moments, is an artistic pursuit. As much as a classically trained ballet dancer is a product of a system, a well trained horse is also a product of a system. But each horse, like each ballet dancer, is also a living piece of art who is unique. In the case of dressage, it is a combination of horse and rider that cannot be reproduced exactly by another. Horses are emotionally expressive creatures; horses are physically impressive creatures; horses are creatures of movement. The tragedy of both ballet dancers and horses is that years of training lead up to a few brief years of peak performance. Fleeting and fragile, we keep the memories and the photos and the videos, but there is simply nothing that can capture what the best moments are like: transcendent.

And, of course, that's what makes it art.

If I Can't be Riding

I always recommend that serious "seekers" go to the www.USDF.org website and download their recommended reading lists. (Go to the Education tab, and then search under both the Instructor/Trainer and "L" program.) It is a worthy goal to develop a library of your own and to have actually read the books in your library. One of the benefits of going through both USDF instructor and judge-education programs is that it forced me to read some books that were not scintillating, but were still important. I had the pleasure of participating in study groups for both of my instructor certification tests and for the "L" exam. We taught each other at the same time that we cheered each other on (and ate junk food).

While I think riders should start their "self-study" project with the USEF Rule Book, and then the German Federation's, "Principles of Riding" and "Advanced Techniques of Dressage," from that base of knowledge riders are ready to branch off in all sorts of different specific topics. By using the USDF reading list, you know the reads have been "vetted" as being mainstream as well as cutting edge. By reading Hilary Clayton, for example, you discover new insights into biomechanics of dressage movements. By reading Susanne von Dietze or Eckart Meyners or Beth Baumert you learn about the biomechanics of seat and position. By reading Jochen Schleese you learn about proper saddle fit. The list is endless and, each time you finish a book, you have engaged and expanded your mind.

I once read that if one read ten books (only ten!) in any field, one would be (compared to everyone else I suppose) an expert. While I know you cannot become an expert in dressage by reading ten books, I also know your riding will be improved from the effort.

In addition to those worthy reads, there are some books that have made big impressions on me as a rider that did not make the official list. Although I am probably forgetting some wonderful books, I list below the ones that came to mind. Remember, these are the ones that were NOT on the USDF list.

Memoirs

Riding Toward the Light Paul Belasik
A Rider's Survival from Tyranny Charles de Kunffy
Taking up the Reins Priscilla Endicott
My Horses My Teachers" Alois Podhajsky

Self Examination/Mental Game

Seven Deadly Sins of Dressage Douglas Puterbaugh
How Good Riders Get Good Denny Emerson
That Winning Feeling Jane Savoie

Others

Dressage for the 21st Century Paul Belasik
(Any books by Charles de Kunffy)
The Dressage Horse Harry Boldt
The Simplicity of Dressage Johann Hinneman /Coby van Baalen
Dressage: A Guideline for Riders and Judges Wolfgang Niggli
Here are some of the videos and DVDS that I have loved. Most of my collection is on VHS, but I expect they can now be found through the internet.
BBC "The Horse in Sport—Dressage" (very hard to find but beautiful and moving introduction to dressage)
Kyra Kirkland series
Reiner Klimke series
Ingrid Klimke: "Cavaletti"
Arthur Kottas series
Conrad Schumacher series
Balance in Movement by Suzanne von Dietze
YouTube (A free source of good stuff)
Janet Foy and Steffen Peters clinic/symposium on the levels (sponsored by ESCTDA)
Any Olympic Games and/or Championships
Any of the USDF FEI Trainer Conferences

Spectating Bucket List
Olympic Games
World Equestrian Games
World Cup Dressage Finals
USEF FEI Festival of Champions
Lamplight USEF Young Horse Championships
Aachen Horse Show, Aachen, Germany

Bundeschampionat, Warendorf, Germany
World Breeding Championships for Young Horses
Olympia Horse Show, London, UK

Publications
USDF Dressage Connections (Essential, and included as part of membership)
Dressage Today (Essential)
The Chronicle of the Horse (Covers multiple horse sports and competition results)
Practical Horseman (Covers multiple horse sports and horse and stable management)

And last, but not least, *The Dressage Chronicles* by this author, Karen McGoldrick
Follow Lizzy and Margot's journeys through four books:
The Dressage Chronicles
A Matter of Feel: Book II of The Dressage Chronicles
The Right Girl For The Job: Book III of The Dressage Chronicles
Rings of Fire: Book IV of The Dressage Chronicles

Left: Ashley Marascalco riding Raphael Rousseau, right: Karen McGoldrick riding Gia, photo by Tyler Hawk | One of the benefits of riding is discovering and connecting with other members of our "tribe." It's been a pleasure and an honor to have dressage trainer Ashley Marascalco "In residence" at Prospect Hill Farm.

Acknowledgments

Thanks as always to Deeds Publishing. Despite not knowing the difference between a half-halt and a half-pass, they have been willing to take the leap into the unknown and publish my books.

Thanks to Ann Genovese founder and director of The Good Horseman Foundation and a USEF rated dressage judge. Ann read every page with care, using both her expertise as a retired newspaper editor and her expertise as a dressage judge. Her critique helped me clarify my thoughts and language.

Thanks to Ashley Marascalco for being willing to be on both sides of the camera to help me finish the project. She and Raphi make beautiful models, but additionally Ashley has an artist's eye and created the photos used on both the front and back covers of the book.

Thanks to all of the photographers for generously allowing me to use their photos. Thanks to Selene Scarsi for the photo she took while I was in Germany. Thanks to Sherry Smith for her shot of my beautiful heartbreaker, Wasabi. Thanks to Tyler Hawk for his early (rainy) morning visit to Prospect Hill Farm to photograph Ashley on Raphael and to photograph my own Gia. Tyler was accompanied by dressage rider Ines Kausche who helped explain to him what it was he was trying to photograph! Thank you Ines.

A general shout out to all who have been supportive of my writing. I'm not famous. I am no guru or horse whisperer. I haven't made any teams or won any important events. I will always be more of a "Lizzy" than "Margot," but I still thought perhaps I could contribute to the body of literature on dressage in ways that I had not seen done. I started this process by deciding to write one novel on dressage and without meaning to, that one novel grew into a series of four books. This final book is a way of giving my riding readers just a little bit more. I hope I made you laugh and feel the difficulties of this life we chose, and along the way, imparted some practical information. If I have done that, then I am satisfied.

About the Author

Author photograph courtesy of Alicia Frese

Karen McGoldrick rides, teaches, and trains dressage at her own Prospect Hill Farm in Alpharetta, Georgia.

She is a United States Dressage Federation certified instructor/trainer; earned her USDF Bronze, Silver, and Gold medal rider awards, all on horses she trained; and she graduated "With Distinction" from the USDF "L" program.

You can visit Karen online at www.thedressagechronicles.com

www.ingramcontent.com/pod-product-compliance
Lightning Source LLC
LaVergne TN
LVHW041334080426
835512LV00006B/458